TEN HOUSES

TEN HUSES

Edited by Oscar Riera Ojeda

Lacroze Miguens Prati

Rockport Publishers, Inc.
Rockport, Massachusetts

First published in the United States of America by:

Rockport Publishers, Inc.

146 Granite Street

Rockport, Massachusetts 01966

Telephone: 508-546-9590

Fax: 508-546-7141

ISBN 1-56494-326-8

10 9 8 7 6 5 4 3 2 1

Cover Photo: House in Gorriti Street / Photo by Gustavo Sosa Pinilla

Back Cover Images (left to right from the top): Pages 18, 59, 79,
23, 65, 79, 23, 65, 91, 42, 73, 99, 44

Printed in Hong Kong

Graphic Design: Lucas H. Guerra / Oscar Riera Ojeda

Layout: Oscar Riera Ojeda

Composition: Matthew Kanaracus / Codesign

Contents

-oreword

by Oscar Riera Ojeda

bridging the gap between architectural erudition and popular culture through the deceptively simple task of designing a house challenges the intellectually ambitious architectural practice. Establishing a common denominator that spurs interest from both a narrow range of architectural cognoscenti and the vast majority of people becomes a difficult and brittle proposition.

Historically, numerous examples of outstanding houses designed by the acknowledged masters of the Modern Movement and their no less illustrious successors, repeatedly were bastardized or humanized—depending on the point of view of the architect or inhabitant—exemplifying the strenuous dichotomy of two seemingly opposite and irreconcilable worlds. "Oh, it's an architect's house..." seems to be the phrase of choice with which the uninterested layman dismisses any space that, by virtue of being far-reaching beyond his most elementary comprehension of "inhabiting," becomes cold and foreign. Confronted with this dilemma, the works of Lacroze, Miguens and Prati successfully establish a bridge that diminishes the distance, transcending issues of style and theory by asserting clarity of thought beyond the circumstantial needs of varying clients and contexts.

Their first houses—unquestionably modern interpretations of popular vernacular typologies— are the breeding grounds of their unmistakable design doctrine: simple but flexible floor plans; precise spatial modulation leading to extreme perceptive clarity; defined boundaries between privacy and community; and unorthodox complexity in the layering of urbanity and rurality. Lacroze Miguens Prati expresses all this within a grammar of easily comprehended, user-friendly domesticity, the hallmark of a practice distinguished by its unambiguous response to the uniqueness of time and place that defines each job.

Respectful of context—both intellectual and technological—the houses of these Argentinian architects achieve their standing through the constant reinvention of the conversational linkage of their components, rather than through mere formal exaltation. The architects orchestrate their meaningful spaces through the dialogue between walls, stairs, chimneys, and patios.

"Good architecture emanates from good clients." Notwithstanding the input of enlightened dwellers who strive to elevate housing from the realm of shelter to the podium of art, the work of Lacroze, Miguens and Prati defies this architectural adage. Regardless of program or context, their skillful handling of architectural basics—light and space, with an understandable idiom—ensures that the gap between layman and architectural cognoscenti always will be bridged. With this the beholder will agree, whether passionate about architecture or not.

This Page: *House in San Martin roof (top), House in El Salado (bottom left), and House in El Talar (bottom right).*

Opposite Page: *House in Olivos.*

Introduction

by Jorge Glusberg

In twenty years of professional practice, the architectural partnership of Eduardo Lacroze, Jose Ignacio Miguens and Francisco Prati achieved widespread recognition both in Argentina and abroad. The firm's body of work searches to rescue dormant traditions and cultural identities from a decidedly regional perspective.

The firm's approach is neither wholly historicist nor wholly grounded in nostalgic nativisms. Quite to the contrary, backed by a commitment to contemporary architectural language, its approach aims at finding the core of architectural meaning and its contextual resonance in theme, time and, most certainly, place. Lacroze Miguens Prati aims to revitalize, not resurrect.

This approach is clearly visible in the ten houses introduced here, although this young firm successfully extends its conceptual reach to larger-scaled projects, heralding substantial and refreshing innovations in a wide range of typologies. The firm deftly and unashamedly extrapolates the guiding principle of rescuing dormant traditions—consistently verified in these simple houses—into the realm of these larger projects. Constituting the basis of an all-encompassing, unifying design system, these ten houses show the genesis of the firm's major non-residential projects, such as resort hotels in Guatemala and Colombia.

The ten houses in this book cover almost fifteen years of search—1980–1995—and, except for the most recent project in Maine, USA, all were built within the boundaries of Argentina. They encompass a rainbow of geographical, cultural, historical and social conditions diverse as the forces that have shaped this veritable Argentine melting pot.

From the flatland pampas of Chascomus (a milestone settlement in the Gaucho Wars) to the rough-hewn Neuquen Andes (outpost of military expansion at the turn of the century) and from the colonial suburbs of Pilar and Olivos to the worker's citadel of Palermo Viejo (Jorge Luis Borges' proclaimed site of Buenos Aires' mythical foundation), these houses stand as silent witnesses to the rich historical tapestry against which they are set.

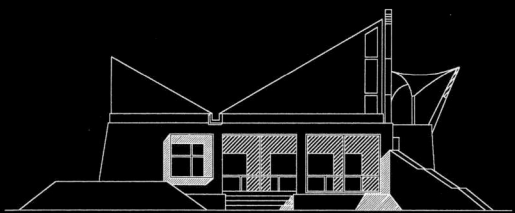

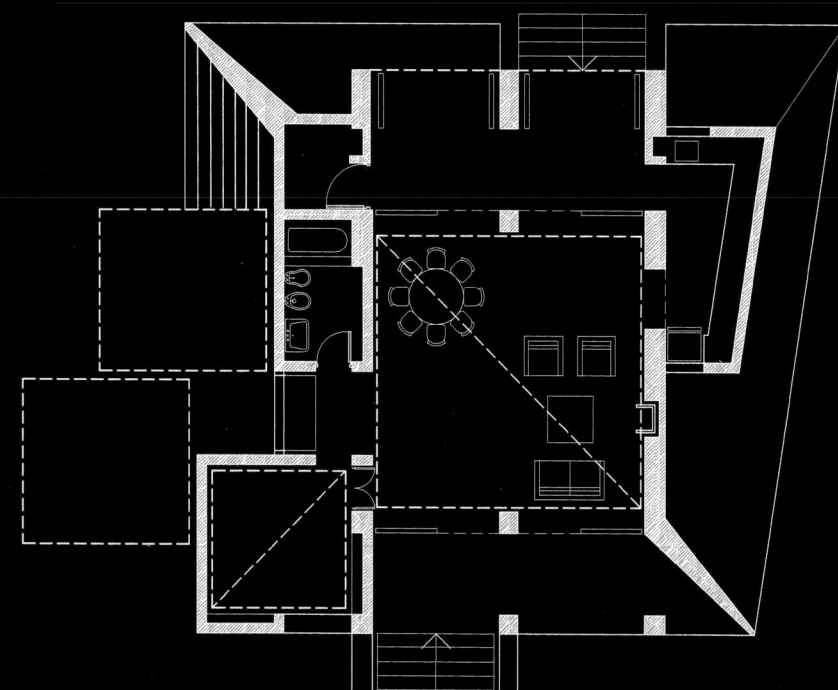

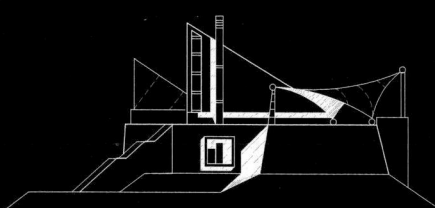

This Page: La Caracola, seven summer-houses, Laguna Garzon, Uruguay, 1987. Conceived as a metaphorical parade of stranded sailboats, these simple structures—an open plan social core with a pinwheeling array of expandable supporting modules—are raised on bermed podiums and capped by windblown rooflines. They are clear examples of the highly iconographical resolution of an otherwise humble program, which, regardless of scale and complexity, is pervasive in Lacroze Miguens Prati's architecture.

Wedged in a granitic Andean ridge's ravine, the San Martín de los Andes house is both cave and turret, simultaneously withdrawn and expansive. Hand-in-hand with technology, the architects boldly appropriated a piece of raw nature—a grass-covered concrete blanket.

The house in El Salado squarely confronts urbanity and rurality. The grass roof fuses with the pampas, an unmistakable gesture of nature taming the intrusion. On the contrary, El Talar makes no pretense of dominance and avoids confrontation, stretching alongside a lagoon and discreetly melting into its surroundings. The age-old vernacular typology—articulating barn and silo—is a thoroughly familiar sight, reminiscent of a thousand settlers' dwellings.

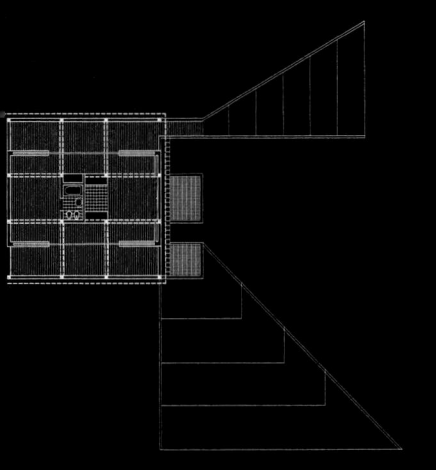

The urban houses—Cabrer, Gorriti, and Carranza—constitute spatial exercises accomplished within the self-imposed boundaries of the *barrio*. Confined behind the anonymity of minimalist facades—a wall and a hole—the Palermo houses spearhead an attempt to recover the essence of neighborhood life. Buenos Aires grew as a continuing aggregate of *barrios*. More than one hundred, a popular song said. Boiled down to forty-six by encroaching zoning laws, they were alive well into the 1960s, when indiscriminate development and zoning prevailed. A few achieved status of honorary republics, and most retain their own historical associations.

Lacroze, Miguens and Prati, through design boldness and technological awareness, successfully breathe modernity into the otherwise stagnant fabric of a neglected *barrio*.

A memento to the past, the Cabrer house maintains the facade of a previous incarnation and engages in elaborate spatial subdivisions with the deliberate recycling of salvage materials. A nod to the future, the Gorriti house strives for spatial totality within its perimetral enclosure, the graphic referral grid. In between, the Carranza house stands as a deliberately voided cube, subsequently and methodically filled as the need arises.

This Page: *La Pedrera, seaside condominiums, Uruguay, 1993. Thirty-two summer cottages, perched on a cliff overlooking the Atlantic Ocean, punctuate the coastline, resorting to a subtly changing palette.*

Opposite Page: *House in Ponta das Canas, Florianopolis, Brazil, 1978. Infusing the imagery and technology borrowed from the surrounding fishing community into a highly flexible gazebo-like open plan, this early exercise shows the way to the firm's approach to design/ build practice grounded in contextual availability.*

Yet one more instance of identity recovery, the house in Olivos features a social bridge spanning bedroom pylons. This project constitutes an awakening nod to the Rio de la Plata, Buenos Aires' historically neglected front yard.

The true meaning of these simple, unpretentious structures—dating back to the 1978 Florianopolis beach house with its marriage of coastal Brazilian imagery and technology—cannot be fully gauged without mentioning a few of the large-scale projects so clearly indebted to them. The detail-rich imagery of the Cardenal Newman chain-link patio housing project in Benavidez, Buenos Aires, infuses individuality into communal living. The spartan austerity of elementary forms at the seaside development in La Pedrera, Uruguay, conversely confers a sense of community to a highly isolated prototype. In both cases, fashion gives way to freshness.

Likewise, the highly iconographical layout of the Camino Real Hotel at Tikal— a metaphorical interpretation of a Mayan settlement overlooking Lake Peten in Guatemala—subtly addresses dwelling scale with cliff-hanging, thatched-hut-like modules. Similarly, the brightly colored, prefabricated-wood-frame Decameron Hotel in San Andres, Colombia, bows respectfully to the time-honored scale fragmentation of Afro-Caribbean vernacular architecture. Monumentality, in both instances, gives way to domesticity.

In this context, the house—the foremost architectural object—becomes a transcending object again and again for Lacroze, Miguens, and Prati. For them, as for Gaston Bachelard, the dwelling is man's most immediate, poetic realm. Its imagery remains forever with its dwellers. More important, the image of the dwellers rests forever with the house.

Jorge Glusberg is Director of The National Museum of Fine Arts, Argentina, since 1994, The Center of Art and Communication (CAYC), since 1972, and The International Committee of Architectural Critics (CICA) since 1978. He is Associate Professor at the Art Department of New York University since 1980, Caballero en la Orden de las Palma Académicas and Caballero en la Orden de las Artes y las Letras, award-ed by the Goverment of France. He is also Doctor Honoris Causa at the University of Lima, Peru, 1981, Honorary Member at the International Union of Architects (UIA) since 1995. Mr. Glusberg is author of more than 25 books on art and architecture. Some of his awards include the Gold Medal for Criticism, Sofia Biennial, 1981; Jean Tschumi Prize for Criticism, UIA, 1982; International Jury for the Center Tete de la Defénse, Paris, 1983; First National Prize 1996, Category History of Art for his book Brief History of Argentinian Architecture.

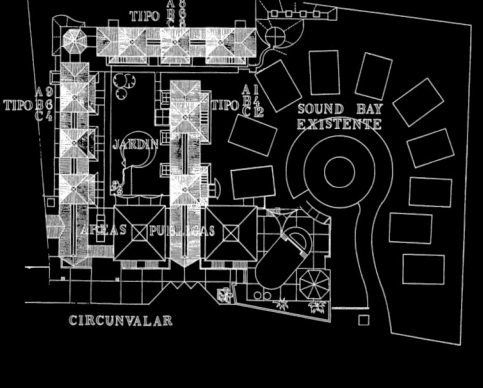

Decameron Hotel, San Andres Island, Colombia

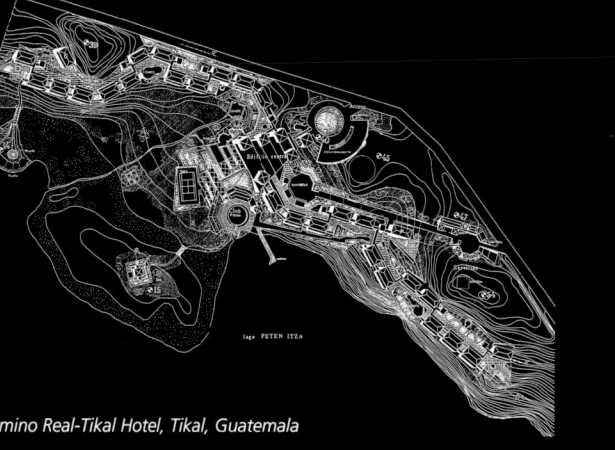

Camino Real-Tikal Hotel, Tikal, Guatemala

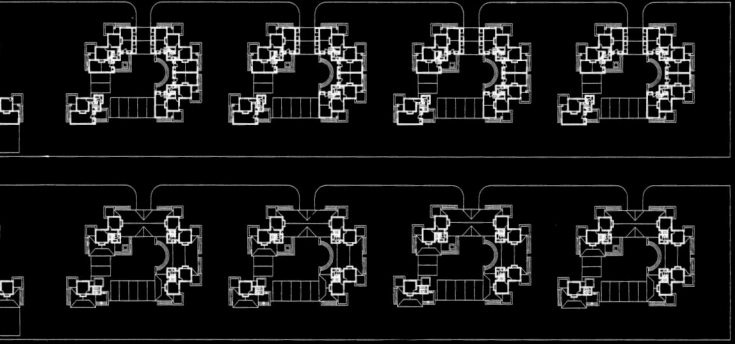

Newman Country Club, Provincia de Buenos Aires, Argentina

House in Maine

Kittery, Maine, USA

A piece of dormant militaria reincarnating as a research scholar's future getaway, this submarine-spotting tower rises from a grassy knoll overlooking the rocky Maine shoreline. In order not to disrupt the tower's well-earned dominance of its surroundings and in order to respect the early Modernist connotations of its design, the renovation allocates functions in a hierarchy that reserves the tower itself to private areas for sleeping and working and relegates the supporting needs—mostly socializing—to the subdued grounds.

The proud undisturbed tower, its distinctive "punch and slit" eyebrowed fenestration unscathed, pivotally emerges from the surrounding berm that anchors a pinwheel arrangement of retaining walls showing a deliberately Miesian recourse with strong proto-modern allegories. Under a grass-covered concrete slab, the walls condense social areas connecting the tower through an underground tunnel contained in a rigid orthogonal grid, a remnant of the original passageway to the artillery embankment.

The retaining walls extend beyond their surroundings, defining space, screening winds, directing perspectives, and confining use. They constitute the only gesture of appropriation of an untamed site. Chimney stacks, flues, and vents project vertically like periscopes, completing the metaphor of a stranded submarine.

Above: Emerging from the rocky Maine shoreline, the WWII submarine-spotting tower, an early Modernist raw concrete structure, dominates the surrounding landscape.

Opposite Page: A horizontal podium, carved into the surrounding mound and opening itself onto the ocean views, tames the grounds while containing the social areas. The tower remains a bastion of privacy.

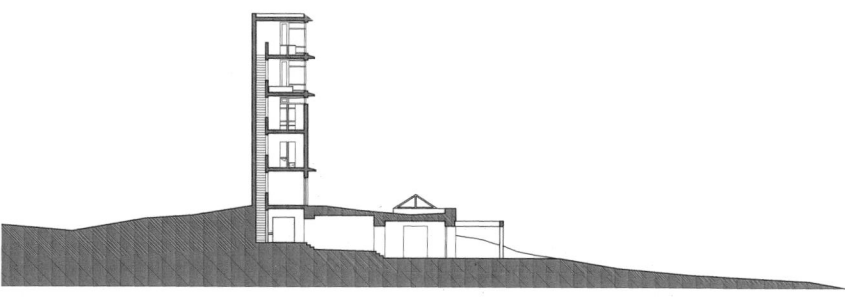

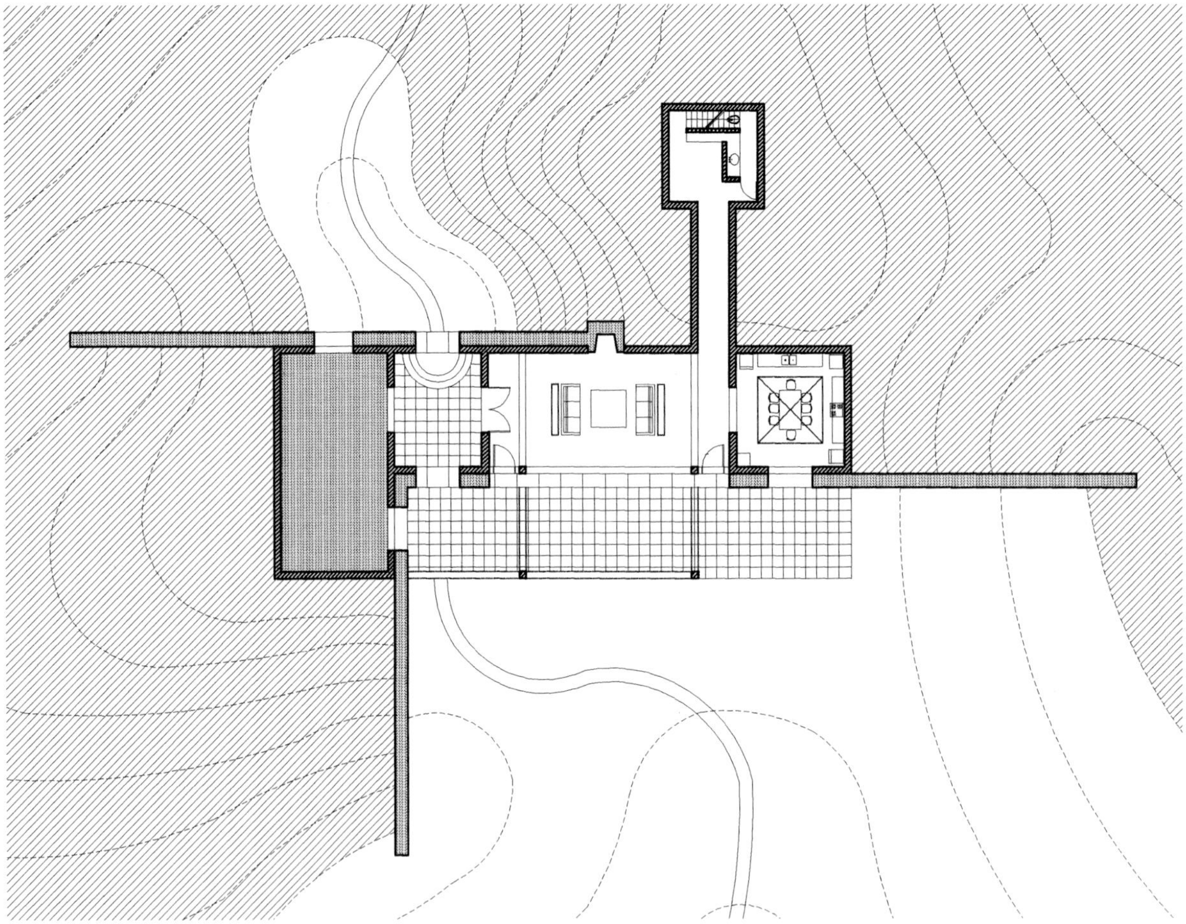

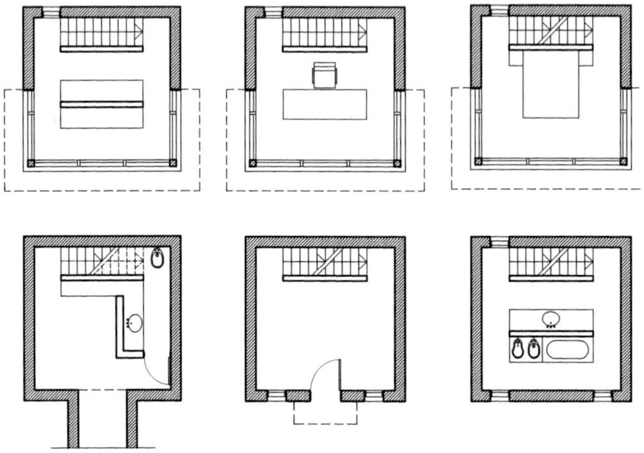

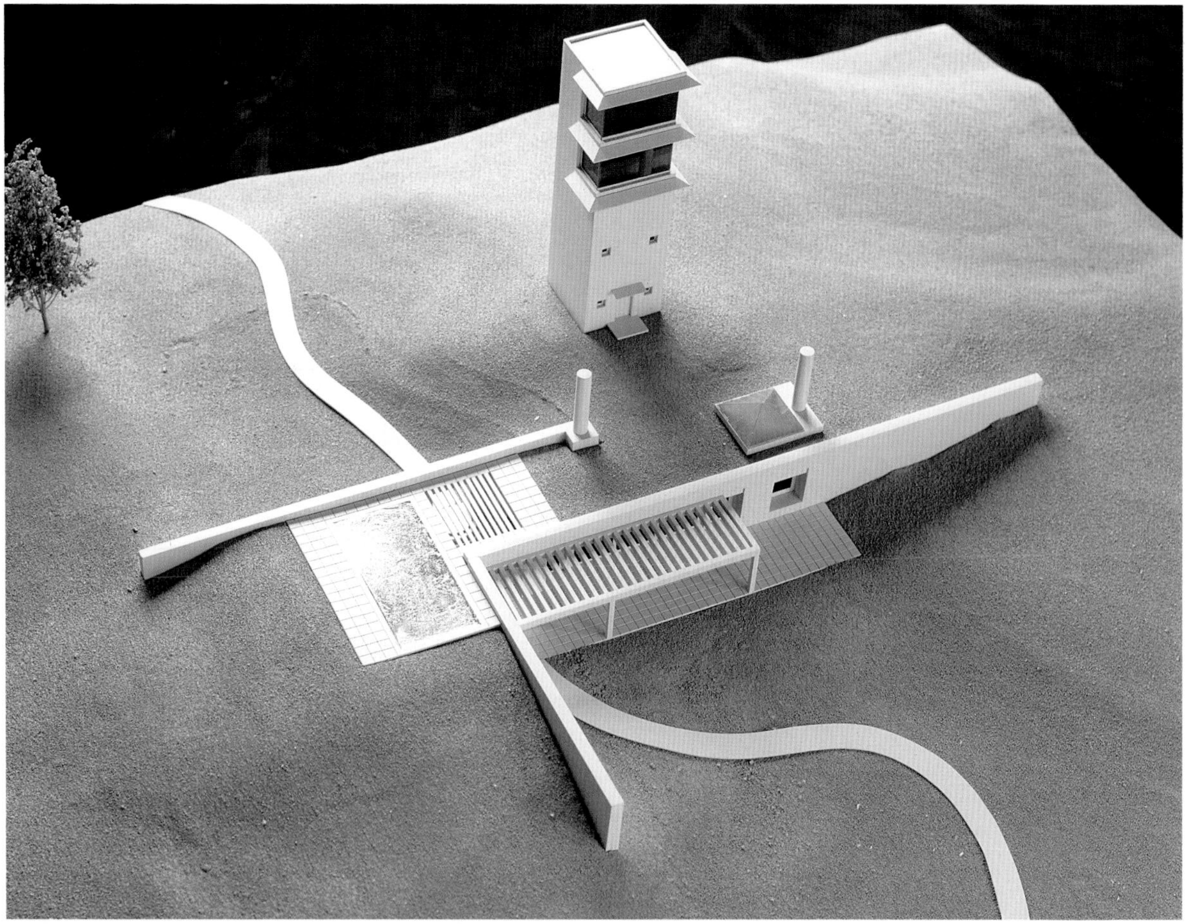

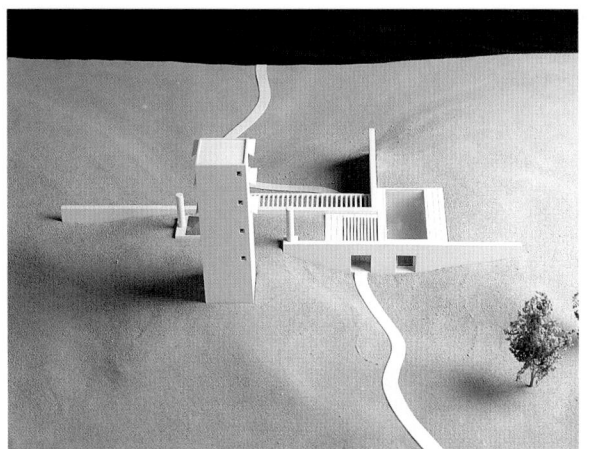

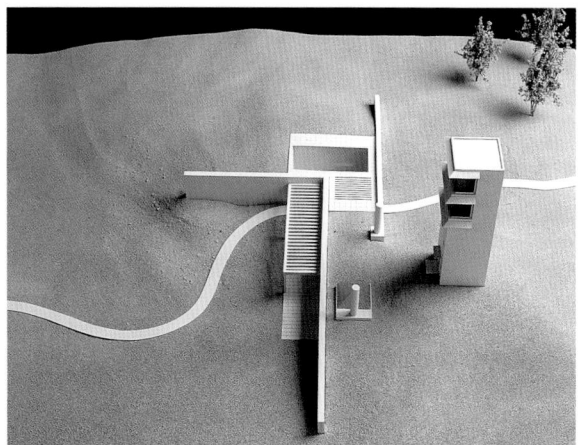

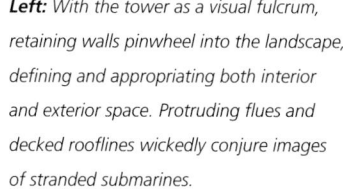

Left: With the tower as a visual fulcrum, retaining walls pinwheel into the landscape, defining and appropriating both interior and exterior space. Protruding flues and decked rooflines wickedly conjure images of stranded submarines.

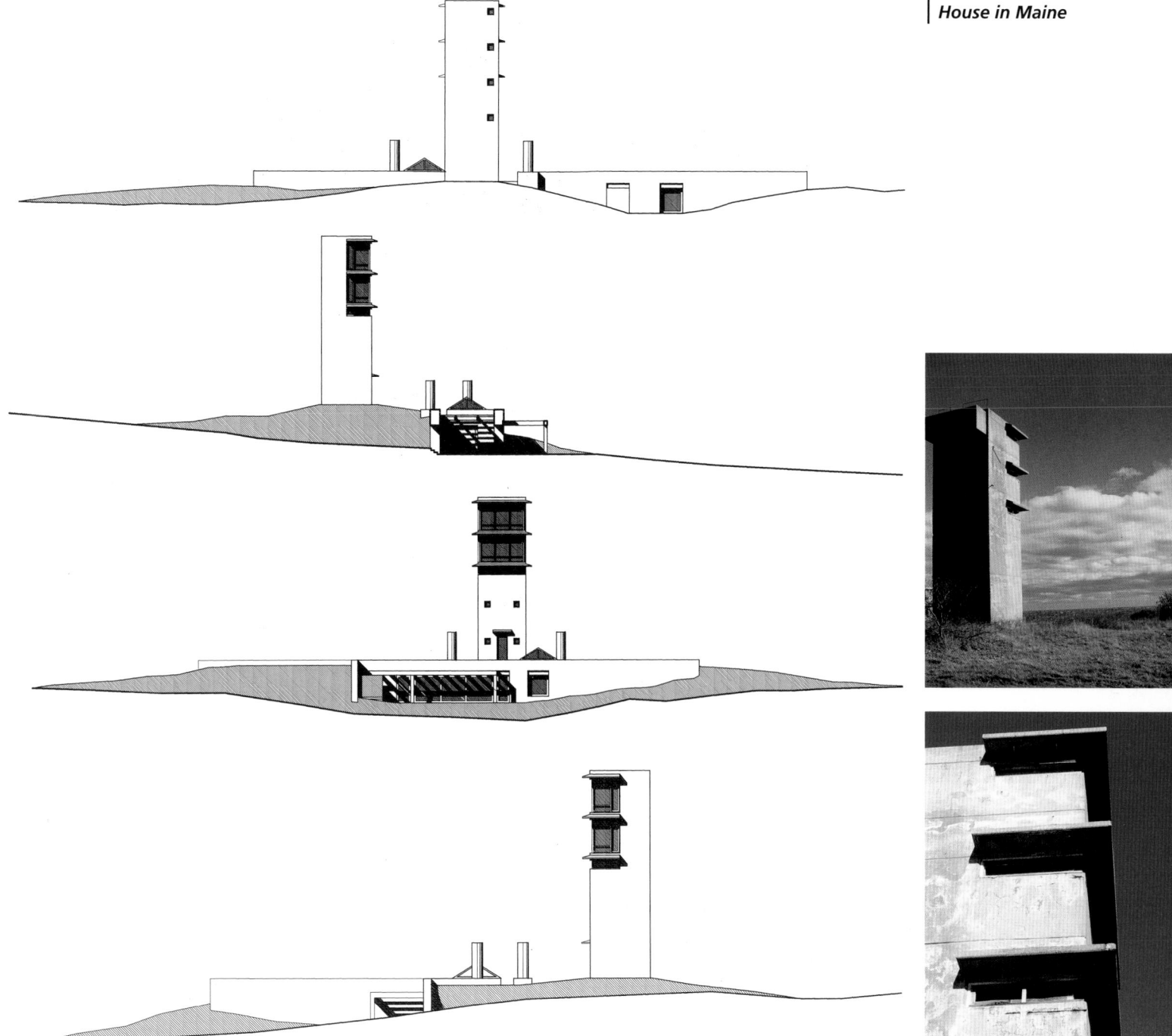

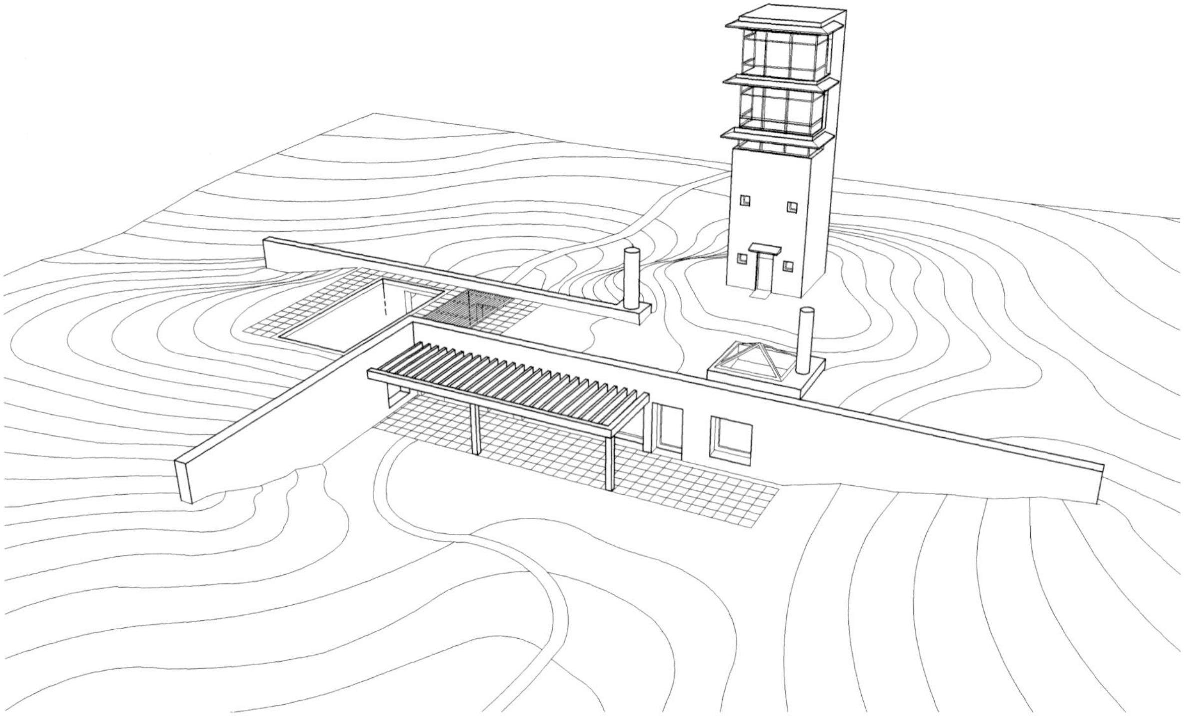

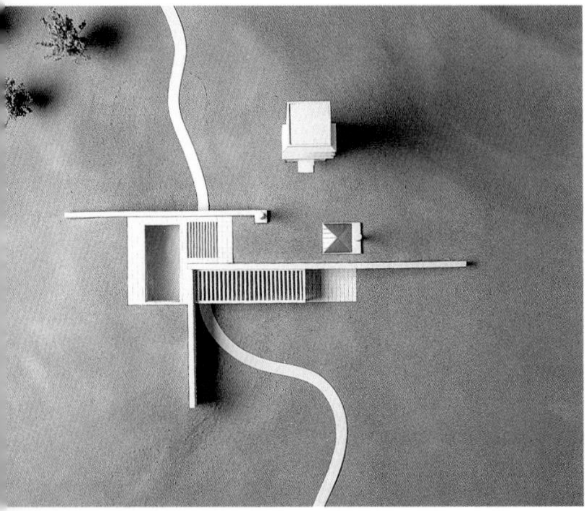

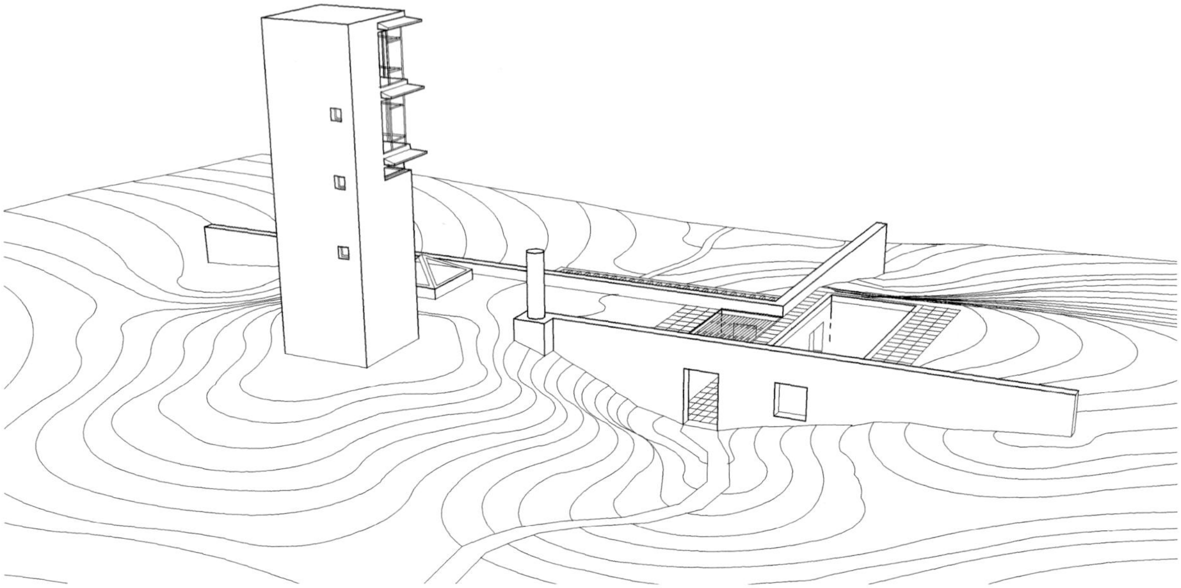

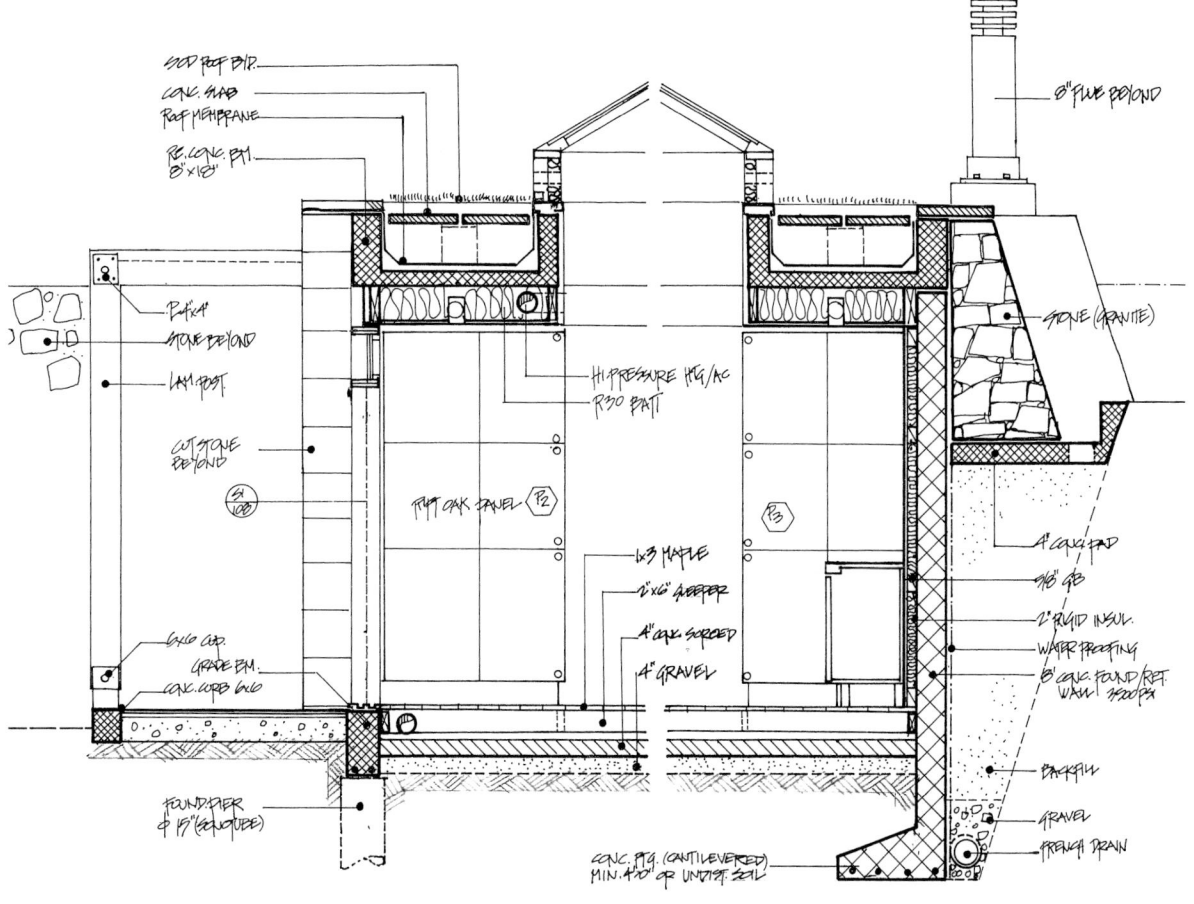

Labels (upper detail):
- SOD ROOF BLD.
- CONC. SLAB
- ROOF MEMBRANE
- RE. CONC. BM. 8"×18"
- 8" FLUE BEYOND
- P.4×4
- STONE BEYOND
- LAM POST
- STONE (GRANITE)
- CUT STONE BEYOND
- HI-PRESSURE HTG/AC
- R-30 BATT
- PLYWD OAK PANEL
- 4" CONC PAD
- 6×6 GB
- 2" RIGID INSUL.
- WATER PROOFING
- 8" CONC. FOUND RET. WALL 3500 PSI
- 1×3 MAPLE
- 2"×6" SLEEPER
- 4" CONC. SCREED
- 4" GRAVEL
- 6×6 COL.
- GRADE BM.
- CONC. CURB 6×6
- BACKFILL
- GRAVEL
- FRENCH DRAIN
- FOUND PIER & 18" SONOTUBE
- CONC. FTG. (CANTILEVERED) MIN. 4'-0" OR UNDIST. SOIL

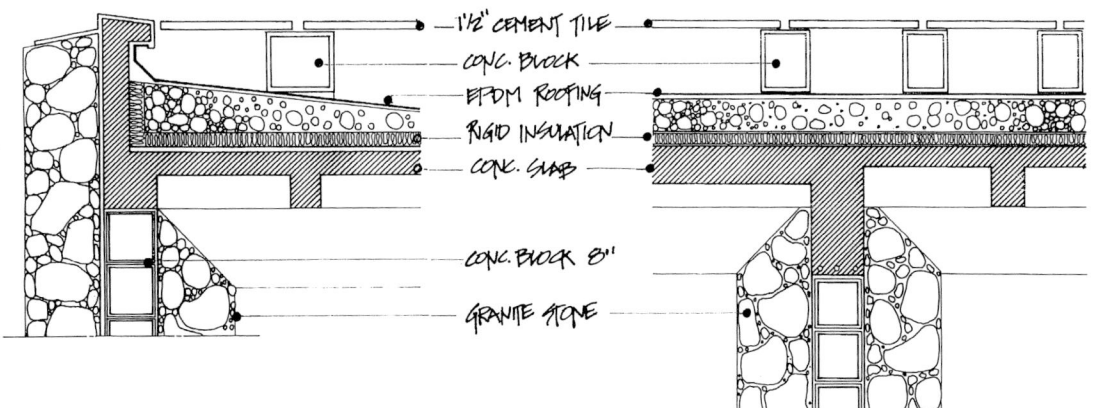

Labels (lower detail):
- 1½" CEMENT TILE
- CONC. BLOCK
- EPDM ROOFING
- RIGID INSULATION
- CONC. SLAB
- CONC. BLOCK 8"
- GRANITE STONE

Opposite Page: *The axial concrete walls gradually fusing into site and stone—and the crisp cedar pergolas floating beyond—are the sole references to the coastal vernacular within an otherwise stark, proto-modern vocabulary. The sod-covered slabs capping the social areas constitute the only carefully manicured expanse in sight. The strong directionality imposed by the emerging walls instills a martial orderliness in consonance with the tower's historical affiliation.*

House in Gorriti Street

Calle Gorriti, Buenos Aires, Argentina

C onfronted with a non-distinctive location—the repetitive, sliver-shaped urban lot—this house constitutes an exploration into reclusive self-containment and spatial implosion. Withdrawing from the featureless surroundings through a blank, pierced front wall that conceals an atrium-like, open courtyard, the house is conceived as a spatial continuum that meanders through a hollowed horizontal prism and is punctuated by service wrappers articulating function areas.

To achieve visual continuity, the service core is totally detached from the load-bearing party walls that penetrate the layering of outdoor/indoor spaces. Axially reverted into a longitudinal parade of decomposed, free-standing elements, the service units become self-expressive. The orthogonal planes are detached from one another, with all intersecting lines dissolved through the use of glass slits that replace the conventional punch-hole fenestration and ensure maximum penetration of light and sight. Individualized and isolated through the use of light and color, a Mondrianesque grid of primary colors reinforces a thoroughly urban and intellectual Kandinskian puzzle of Point, Line, and Plane. Concept, as translated by color with the help of light, becomes the primary expressive vehicle. Self-effacing, quasi-industrial detailing—seamless surfaces, steel girders, and exposed concrete—reinforce the message of choice within a budget.

Above: *The front patio—a veritable outdoor atrium—sets the approach to the stark symmetry of the second-tier facade.*

Opposite Page: *Detached from the immediacy of its enclosure by a perimetral glass slit, the rear wall stands archwaylike as a transition between indoors and outdoors, framing, vignettelike, the highly structured interior.*

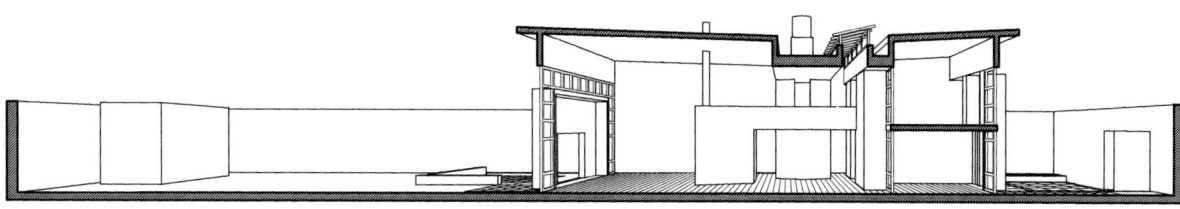

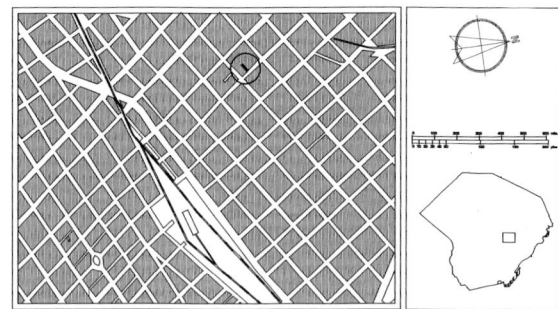

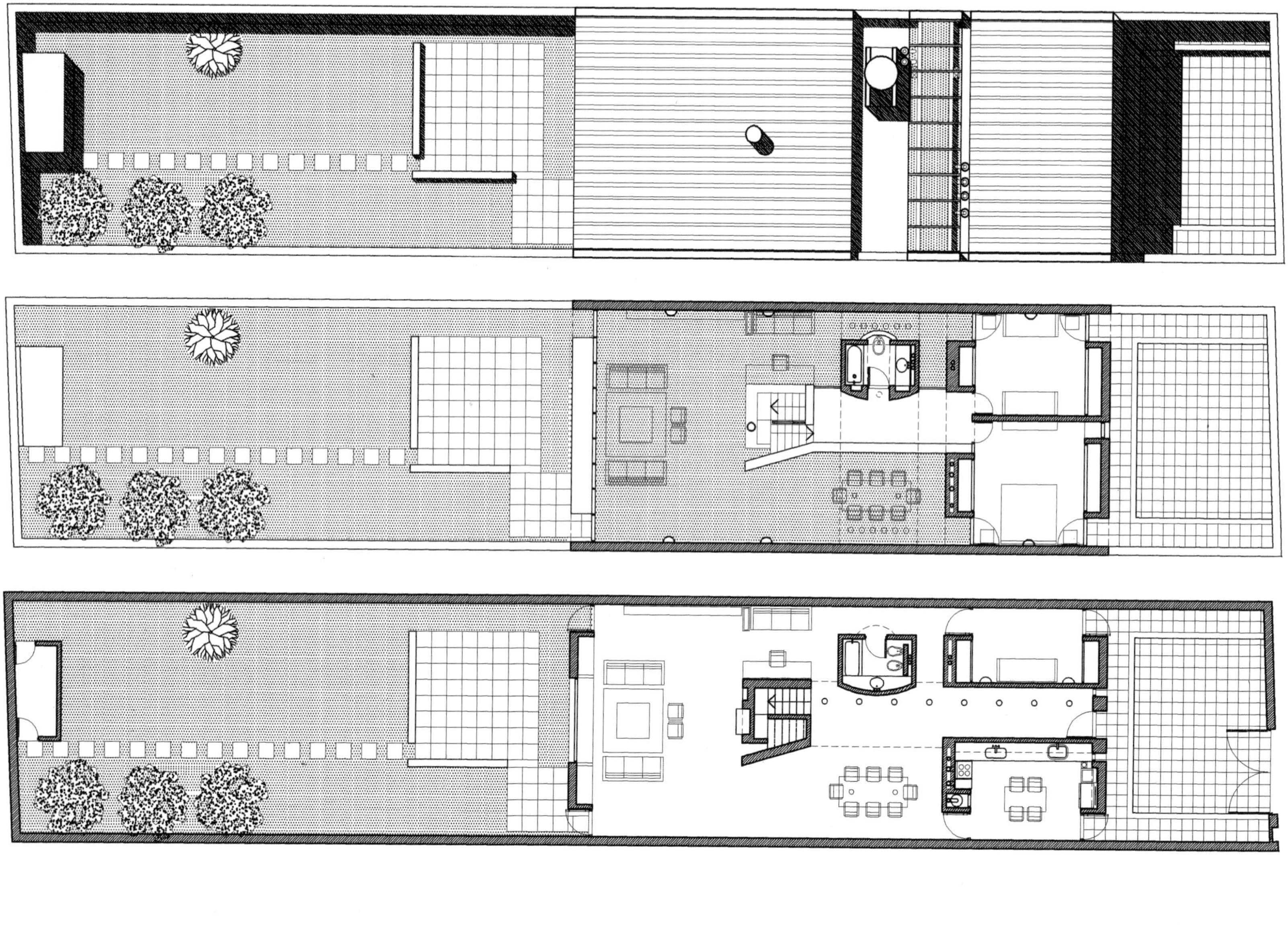

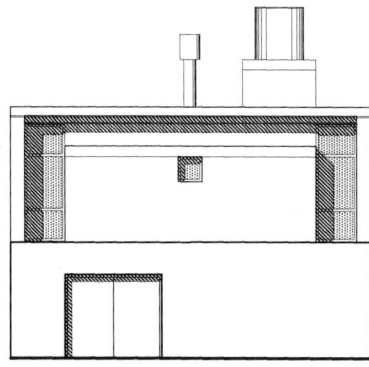

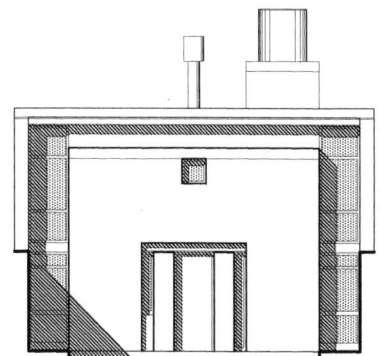

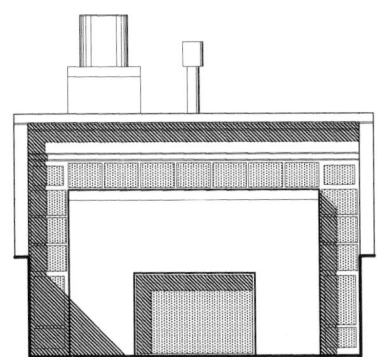

Left: *The modular fenestration, including the wraparound ribbon windows, strictly emphasizes the freestanding quality of the inner sanctum facades, to be understood more as constituent planes of the interior than as enclosure barriers from the exterior.*

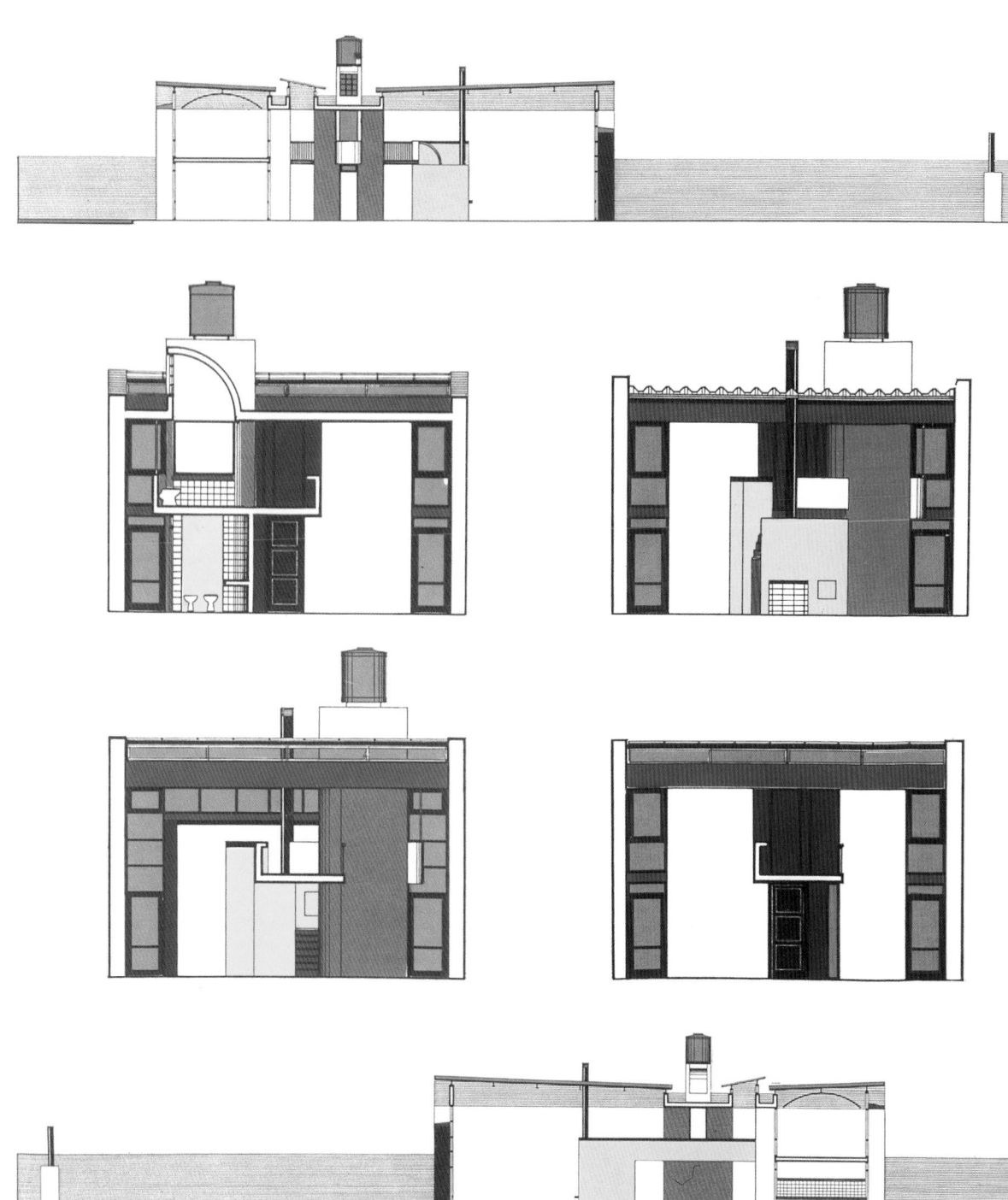

Opposite Page: *The service core is decomposed into a Mondrianesque grid of intersecting planes, their primary colors set against the flowing continuum of the confining party walls.*

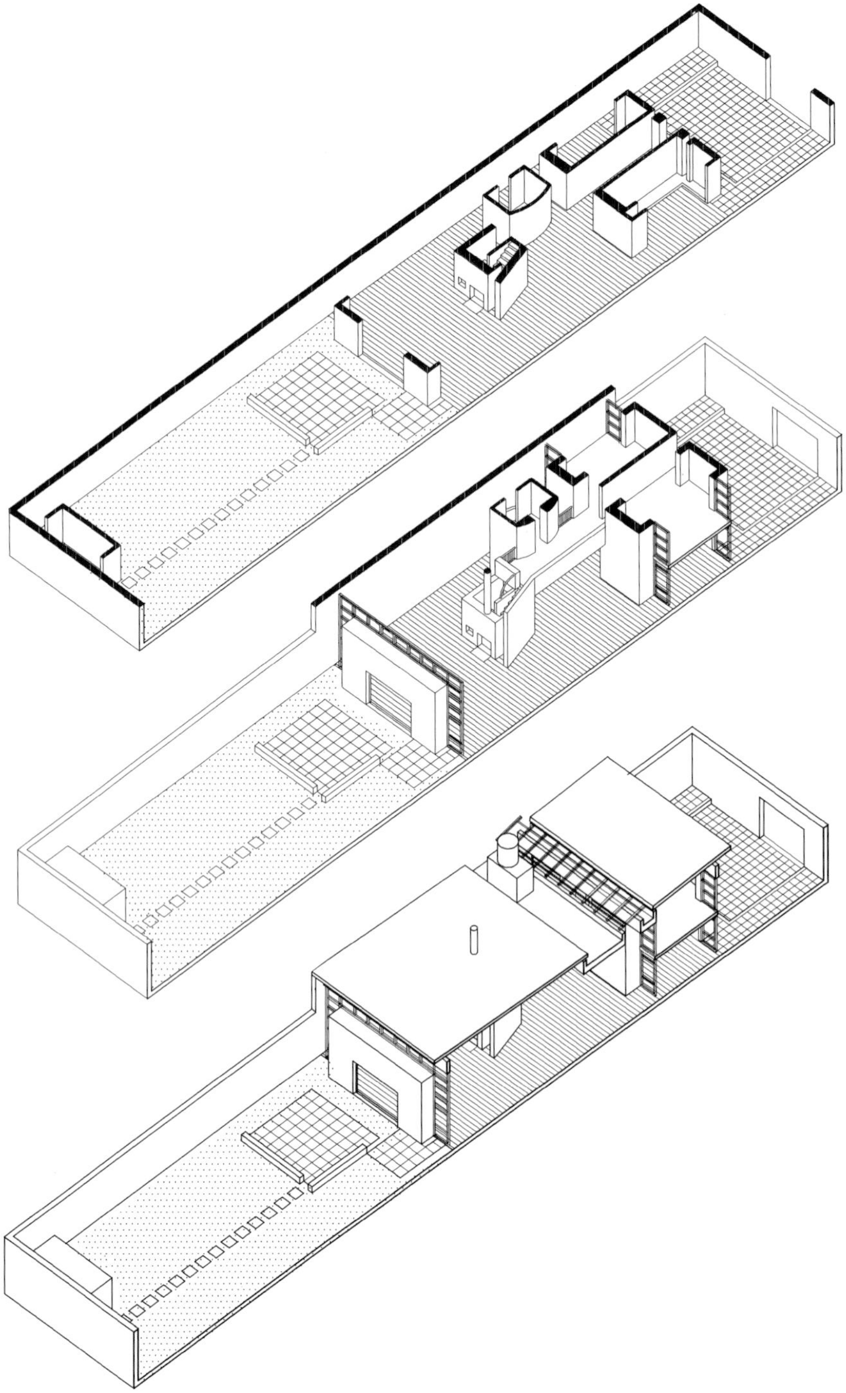

Previous Page and Right: *Within the constantly changing vignettes proposed by the ongoing spatial promenade, the distinctive contours of award-winning designer Diana Cabeza's furniture become referential icons. Form, texture and color infuse domesticity into the conceptual rigors of a complexly layered spatial structure.*

DET. @ ROOFLINE
1. GALV. FLUE
2. FLSHG COLLAR
3. GALV. ROOF
4. SPRAY INSUL. 2"
5. STEEL GIRDER - FN1 12
6. MEMBRANE
7. RIGID INSUL. 1"
8. CONC. SLAB (EXP.)
9. EXP. CONC. (BEYOND)
10. LINE of STUCCO (BYD.)
11. HALOGEN

DET. @ STAIRWELL
12. ∅2" ST. HANDRAIL
13. BRICK PARAPET
14. CONC. SLAB (EXP.)
15. 2¼" FIR FLRG.
16. RADIANT HT. SLAB
17. STUCCO (BYD.)
18. ¾" WD. TRD.
19. CONC. STAIR SLAB
20. CONC. FTG.
21. LINE of WBFP (BYD.)

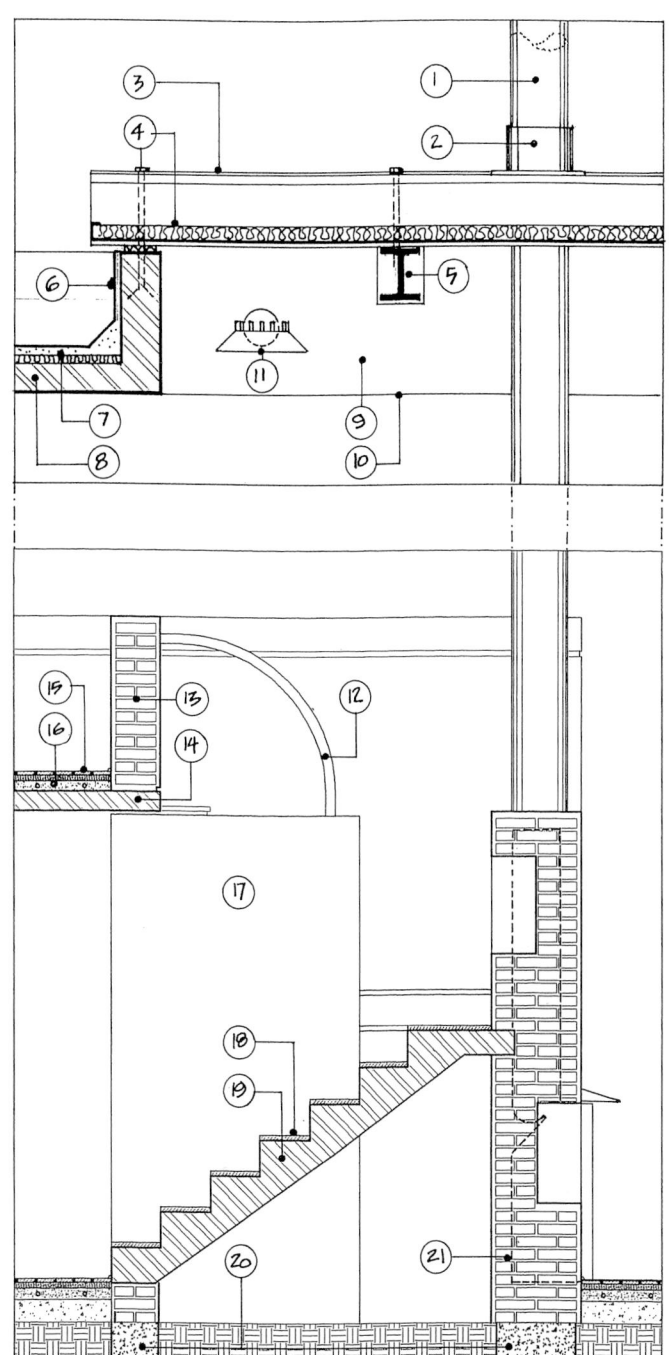

House in Carranza Street

Palermo Viejo, Buenos Aires, Argentina

Set on a deeper-than-usual urban sliver lot and constructed within the constraints of a tight budget, this house was envisioned as a linear succession of indoor and outdoor spaces designed to meet the needs of a young couple. The resulting program deliberately broke down into two independent living units: house and study/poolhouse.

The house—a glass enclosed cube tucked halfway into the lot and wedged between party walls containing a two-tiered package of cooking and sleeping trays overlooking a hollowed out main void—is resolved conceptually as the interaction of Mondrianesque grids defined by the visual layering of fenestration and planar intersections (walls / floors / ceilings). Deliberately superimposed and underlined by a soft palette that emphasizes the blurring of defined boundaries, the visual layering achieves a degree of perceptive ambiguity. This renders scaleless the compressed space—thus making it boundless. The roughly textured, bow-fronted fireplace emerges as the visual fulcrum of this compressed space.

The pavilion-like study incorporates the pool within its roof terrace, providing a controlled visual backdrop and a functional extension of the rear garden while avoiding blight created by an empty pool during the winter. In contrast, the front yard acts as an overscaled welcome mat: screened by a transitional wall framing the main cubicle in a gesture of uplifting grandeur, its directionality is underlined by a guiding steel curb.

Above: An industrial curtain gate cut into a nondescript wall acts both as screen and gateway, providing anonymity and transition.

Opposite Page: Encased between free-flowing party walls, the gridlike precision of the Albertian facade instills a measure of control to the continuum of the patio.

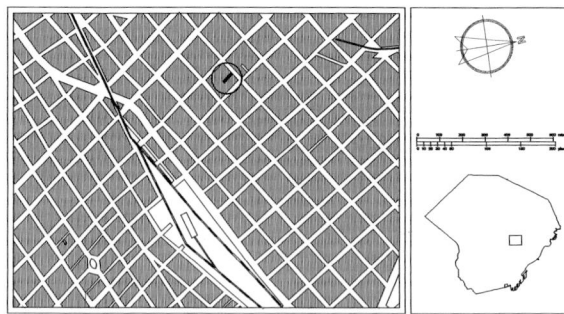

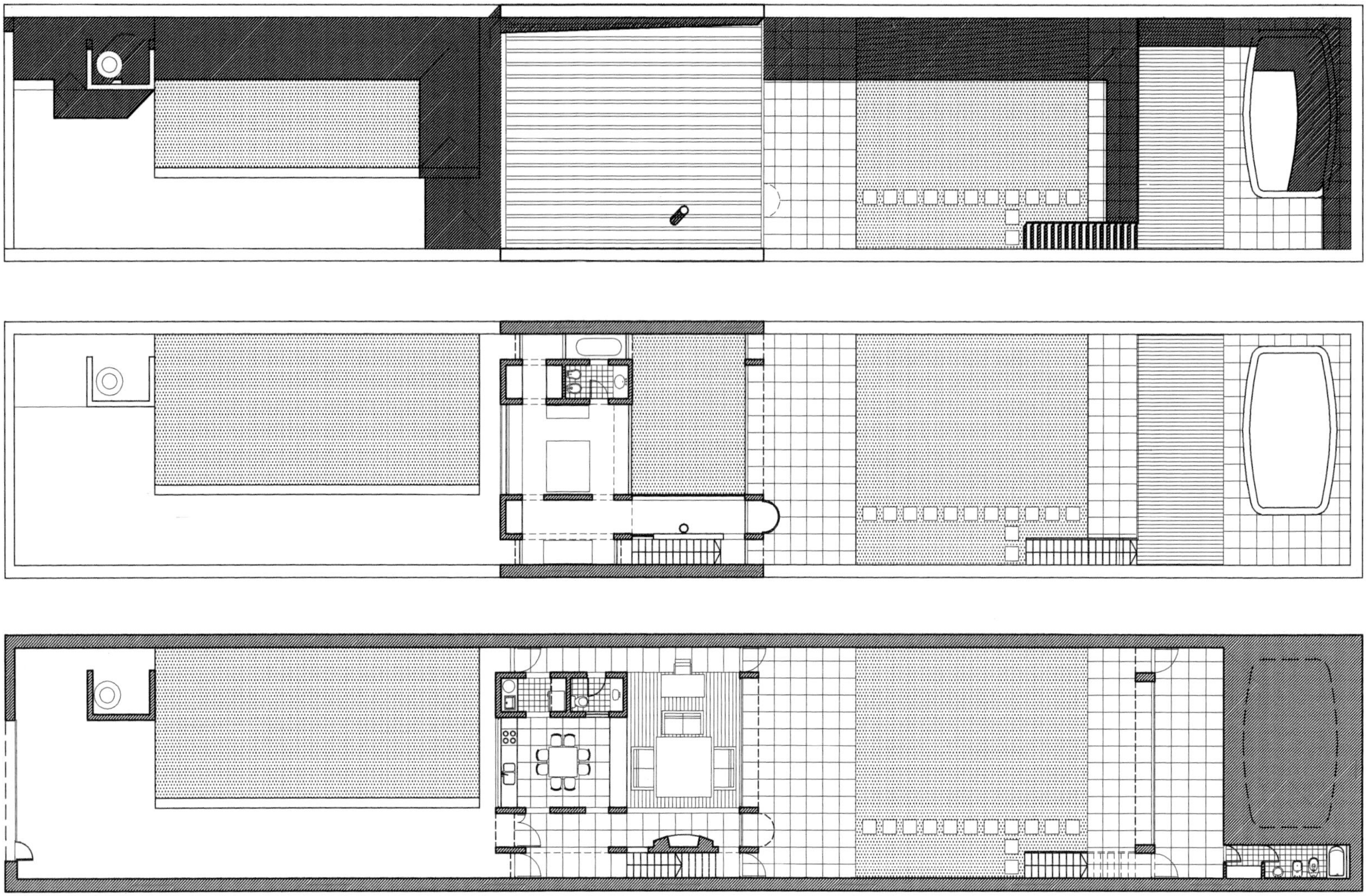

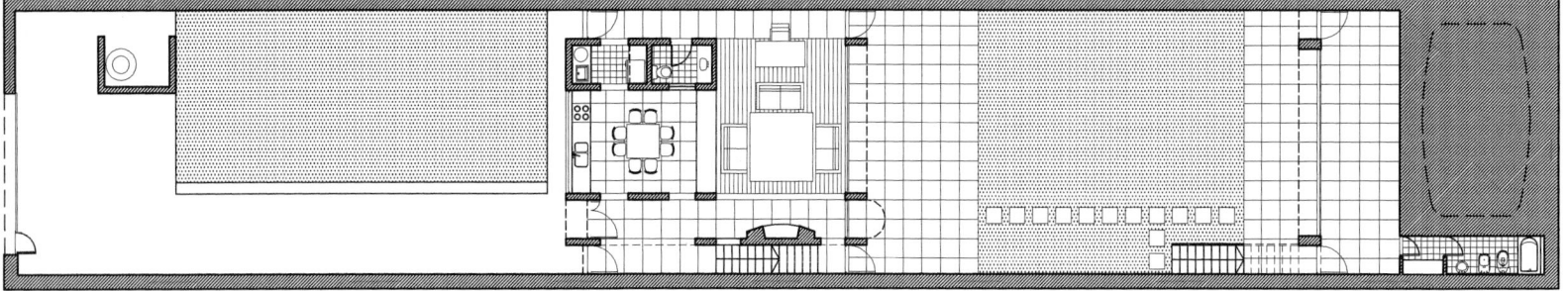

Above: *The rigid geometry of the steel-framed glass wall becomes the only reference of an interior-exterior boundary.*

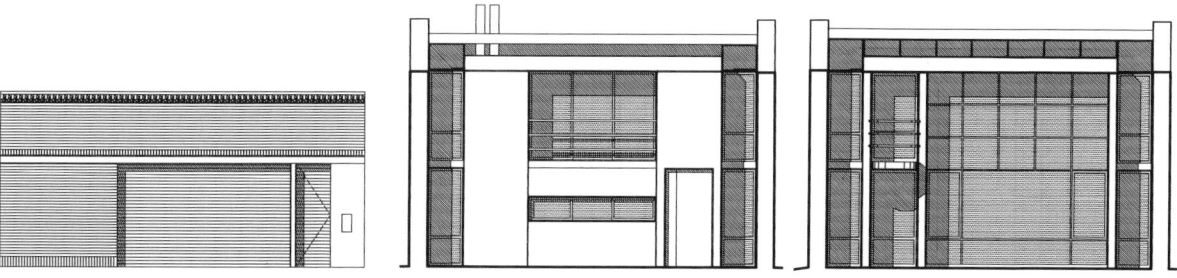

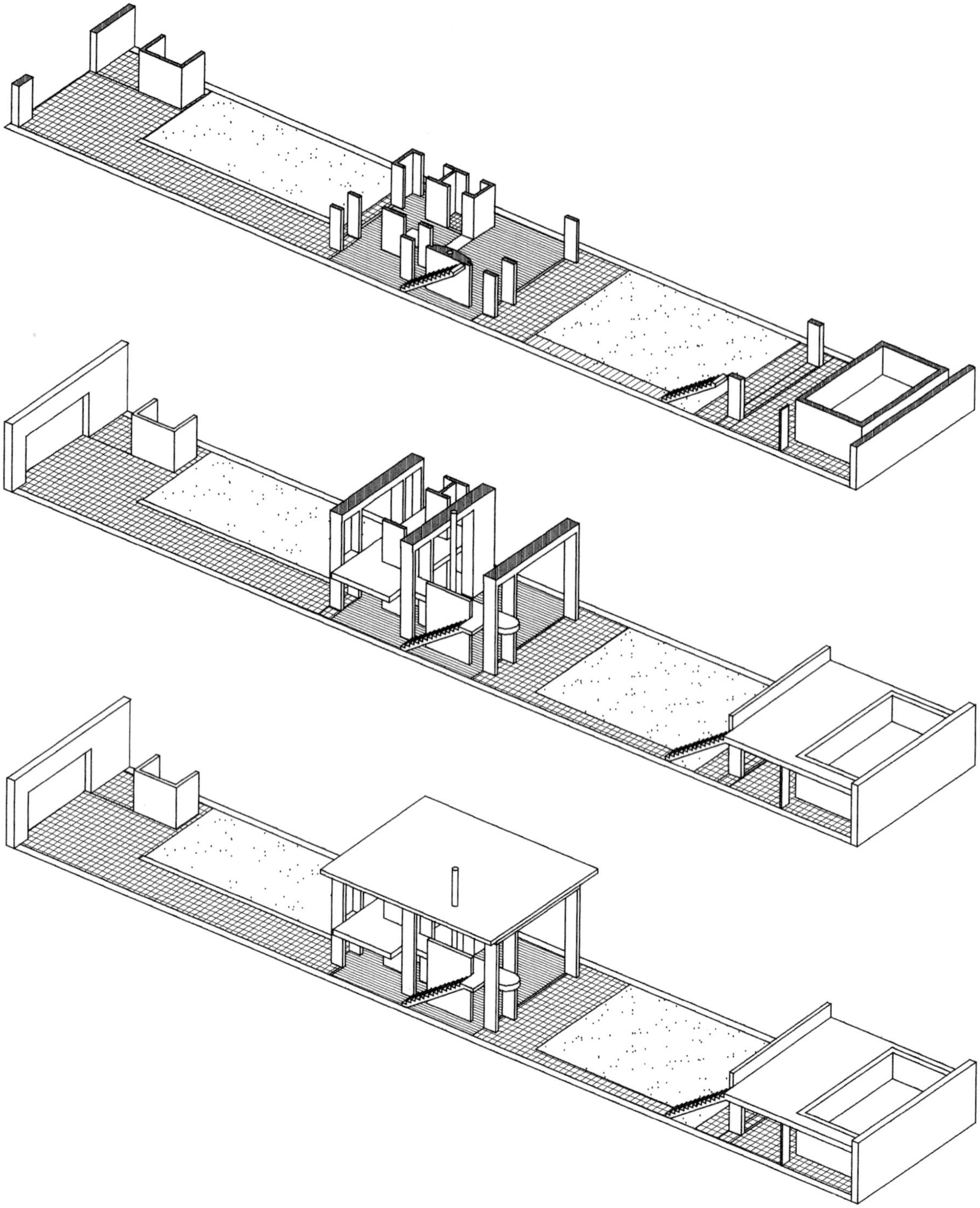

Previous Page and Right: *The coarsely textured brick fireplace and its brightly colored flue boldly pierce through the pastel walls and light-flooded voids, firmly stressing the homely hearth as the house's visual and emotional fulcrum.*

Opposite Page: *The superimposition of referential grids introduces a degree of ambiguity that simultaneously expands and contracts the spatial readings, creating illusory perspectives that enrich the visual experience of the otherwise modest cubicle.*

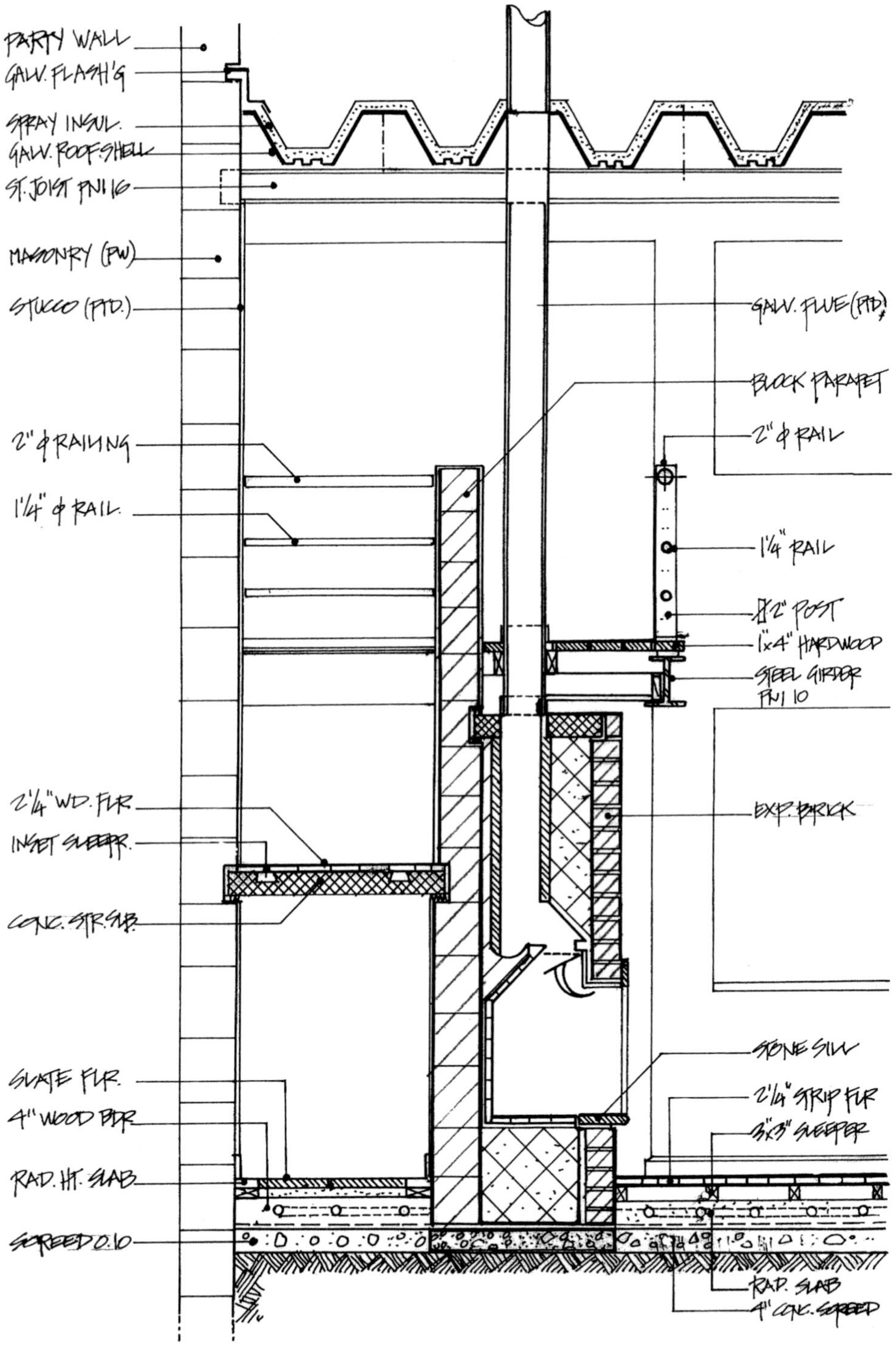

PARTY WALL

GALV. FLASH'G

SPRAY INSUL.

GALV. ROOF SHELL

ST. JOIST PNL 16

MASONRY (PW)

STUCCO (PTD.)

GALV. FLUE (PTD.)

BLOCK PARAPET

2" ⌀ RAILING

2" ⌀ RAIL

1'¼" ⌀ RAIL.

1'¼" RAIL

8"2" POST

1"x4" HARDWOOD

STEEL GIRDER PNL 10

2'¼" WD. FLR.

EXP. BRICK

INSET SLEEPR.

CONC. STR. SLAB.

STONE SILL

SLATE FLR.

2'¼" STRIP FLR

4" WOOD BDR.

3"x3" SLEEPER

RAD. HT. SLAB.

SCREED O.10

RAD. SLAB

4" CONC. SCREED

House in Cabrer Alley

Palermo Viejo, Buenos Aires, Argentina

Straitjacketed into a typical, low-density *barrio* lot that spills onto an underscaled urban alley and includes the remnants of an abandoned structure, the Cabrer house attempts to resolve the choreography of space, light, and technology normally reserved for freer settings.

By condensing all service areas into a transversal, two-layered, multi-tiered, vertical wall plenum—a perforated stack of exposed brick—the house internalizes the concept of enclosure, and frees the perimeter to absorb the impact of colliding site conditions. The street facade is disengaged; the plenum seamlessly weaves into the neighboring visual fabric. The rear, contrastingly resolved as a glazed curtain wall, fuses house and garden into a continuous visual unit. The plenum becomes an internal facade, recreating the outside urban component. Rising unencumbered for the full three stories, it is in fact a vertical architectural promenade hinging—functionally and visually—a succession of open-space platforms resolving the program's space needs.

Brick and wood, painstakingly salvaged from the structure that previously stood on the lot, introduce a familiar range of color and textures that infuses domesticity, renders comprehensible a complex spatial experience, and validates the use of labor-intensive technology when budget constraints are paramount.

Above: The original street facade was zealously preserved, a witness to a previous existence that helps maintain the unusual scale of the alley.

Opposite Page: Towering over the expansiveness of the social curtain wall, the cantilevered concrete balcony guards the private rooms that overlook the adjacent rooflines.

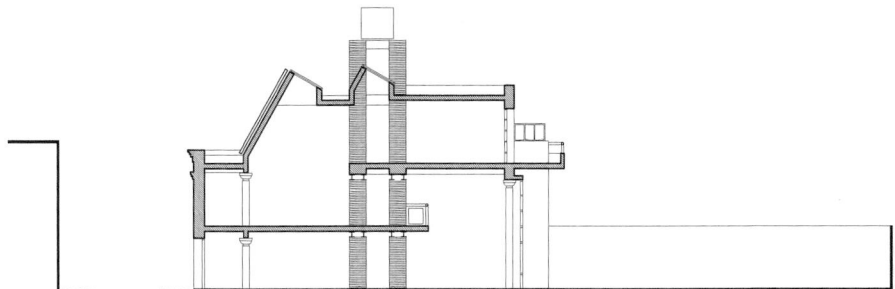

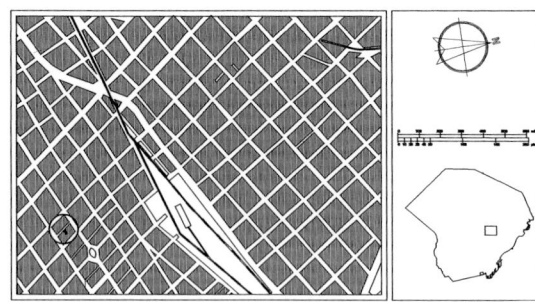

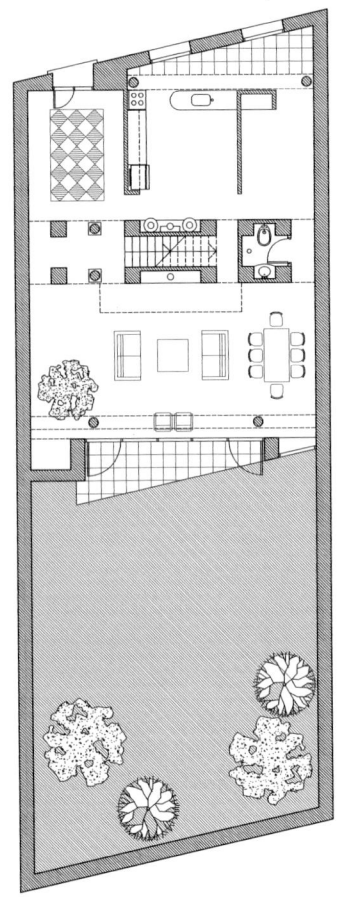

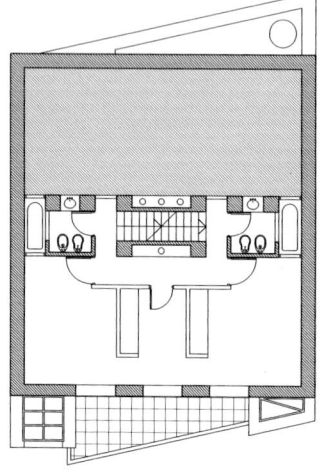

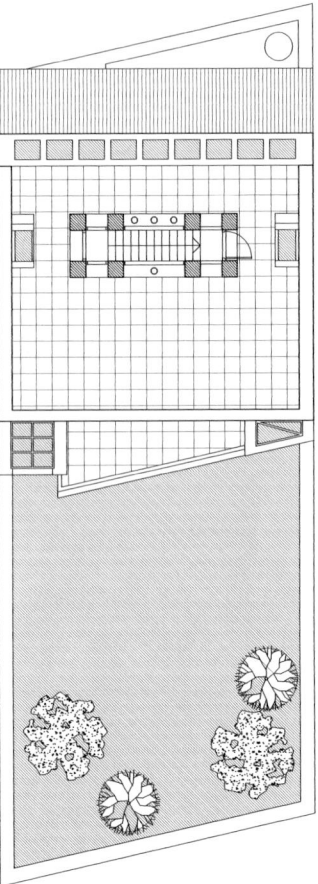

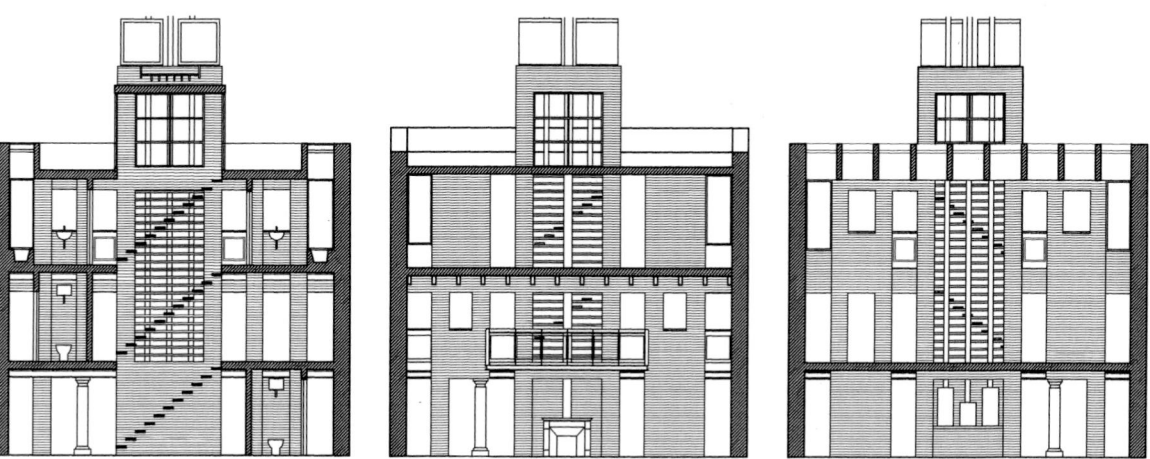

Left and Next Page: *Exposed brick and steel define the character of the double-layered core wall which, visually detached from the flanking white plastered party walls, rises unencumbered. They articulate, right and left in ascending alternating order, the sequence of floor slabs which resolve the functional program.*

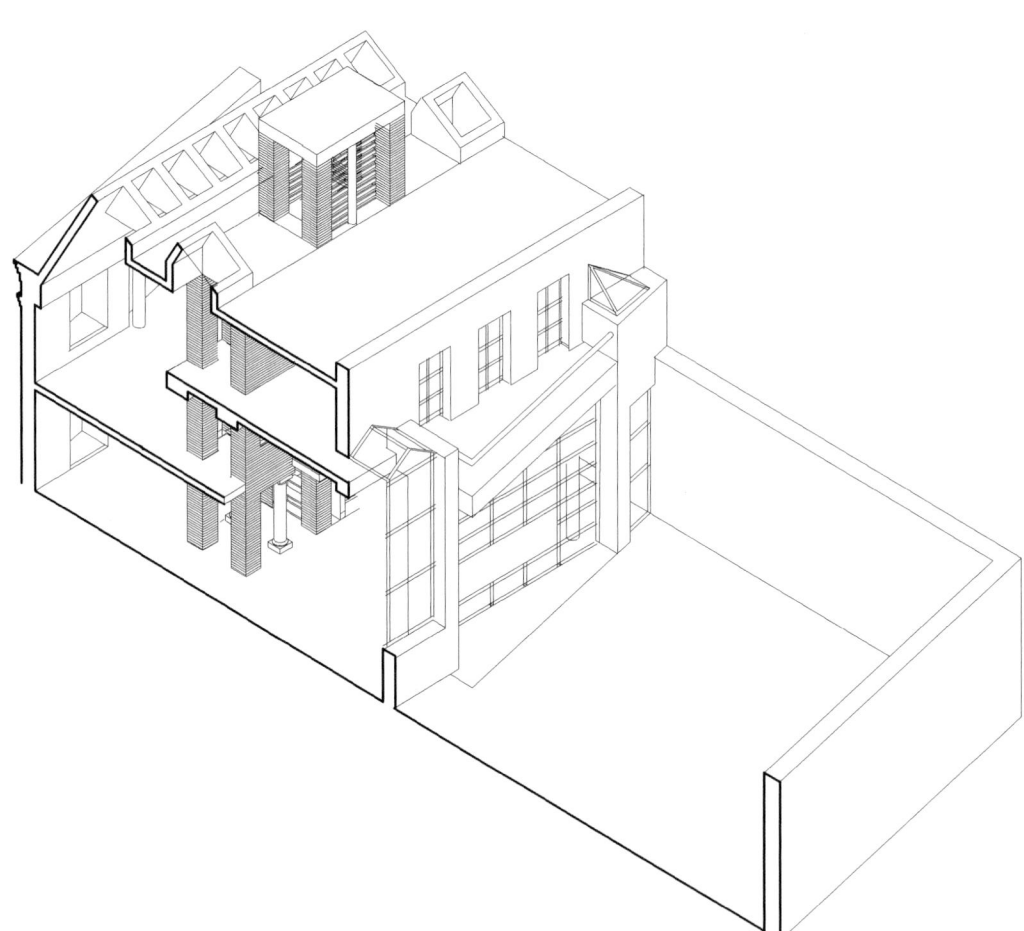

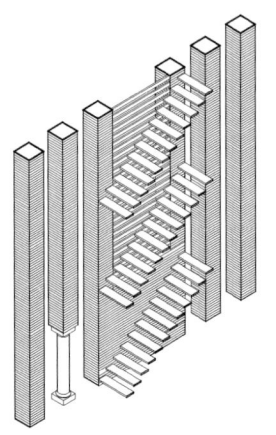

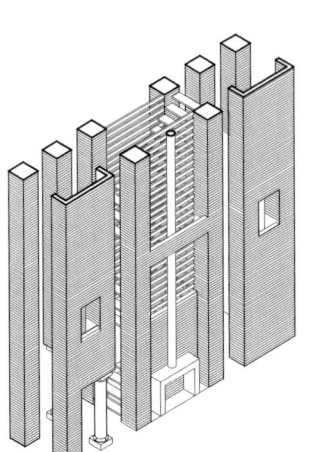

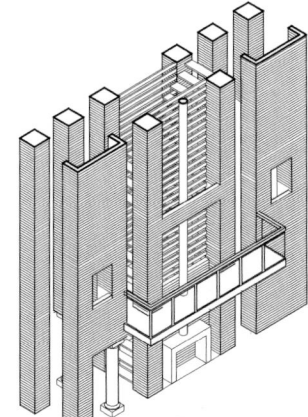

Previous Page: *Wood beams, hand-molded brick, and weathered steel were salvaged from the original construction and reincarnated into the lexicon of urban rurality, which this house openly embraces. The boldness of Jorge Michel's wood sculpture, serenely assertive, seamlessly blends into this exercise of light and texture.*

This Page: *The tile-and-marble Victorian stove is axially centered in the nave-like social room that fully spans the width of the lot, punctuated by the elongated concrete columns that double as visual portico to the rear garden.*

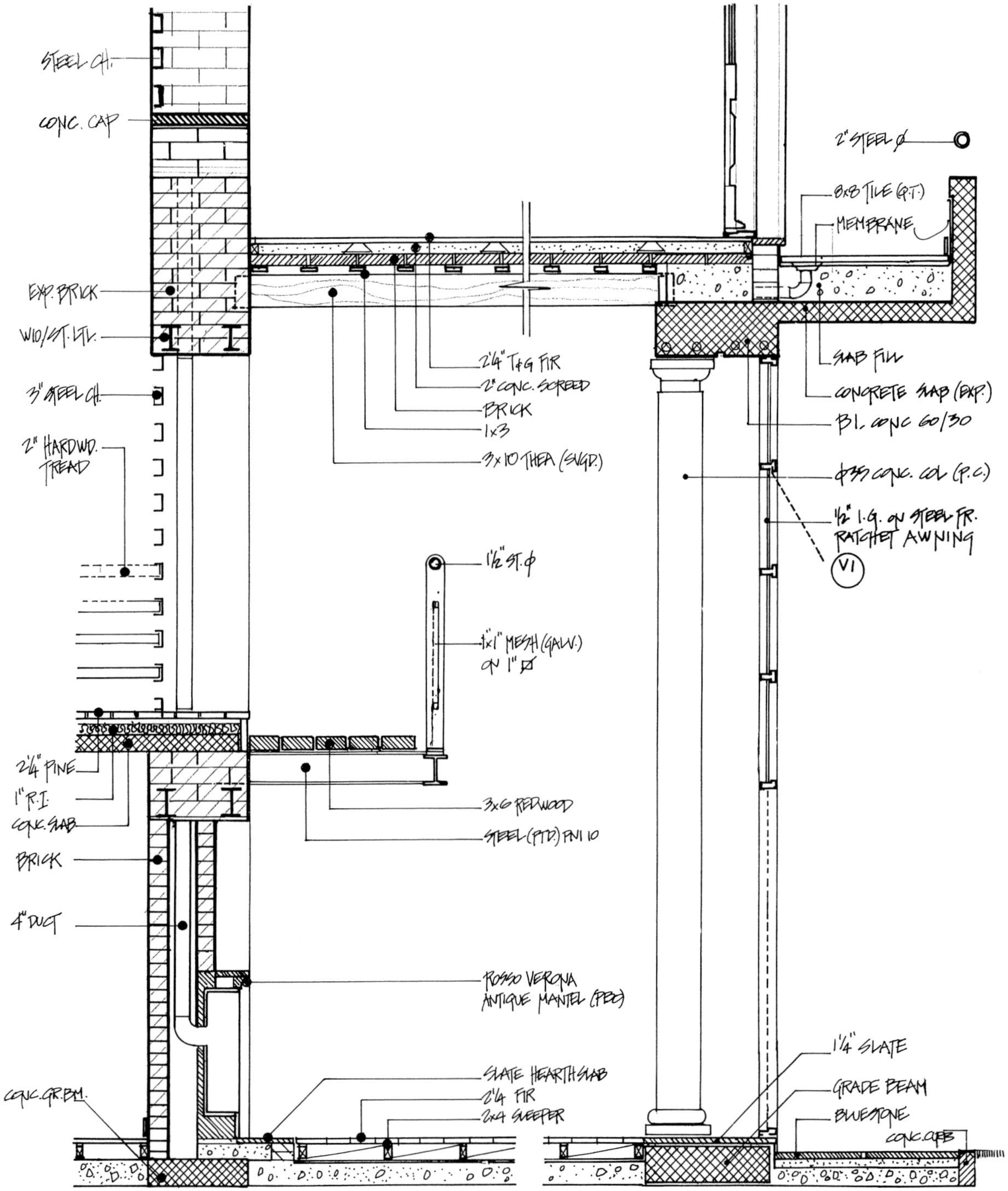
STEEL CH.
CONC. CAP
EXP. BRICK
W10/ST. LTL.
3" STEEL CH.
2" HARDWD. TREAD
2¼" PINE
1" R.I.
CONC. SLAB
BRICK
4" DUCT
CONC. GR. BM.
2" STEEL Ø
8x8 TILE (Q.T.)
MEMBRANE
2¼" T&G FIR
2" CONC. SCREED
BRICK
1x3
3x10 THEA (SLVGD.)
SLAB FILL
CONCRETE SLAB (EXP.)
BI. CONC 60/30
Ø35 CONC. COL (P.C.)
½" I.G. ON STEEL FR. RATCHET AWNING
V1
1½" ST. Ø
1x1" MESH (GALV.) ON 1" Ø
3x6 REDWOOD
STEEL (PTD) PN1 10
ROSSO VERONA ANTIQUE MANTEL (PEC)
SLATE HEARTH SLAB
2¼ FIR
2x4 SLEEPER
1¼" SLATE
GRADE BEAM
BLUESTONE
CONC. CURB

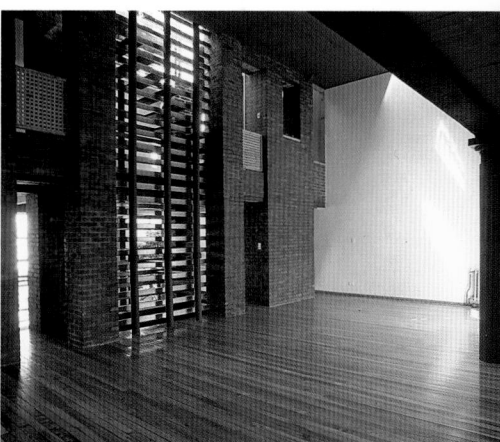

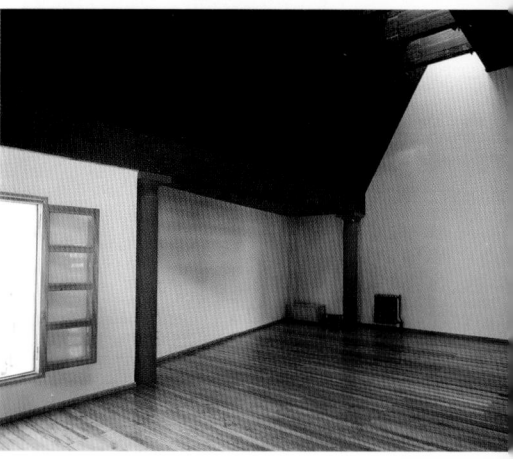

House in San Isidro

San Isidro, Buenos Aires, Argentina

E merging with gridlike precision from a foundation slab floating on infill land, the twelve pairs of load-bearing brick piers that comprise the San Isidro house illustrates how, early on, the firm structured a clearly organized spatial grid that resolves a residential program's functional and contextual problems at a given location and within a certain technological range.

The double rows of matched piers, running the length of a rationally orthogonal slab, constitute individual space organizers. They conform, with graduated degrees of opacity, flanking galleys that alternately resolve functional needs and contextual demands. To the north, a double-tiered system of louvered verandahs generates a climatic buffer that screens indoor spaces from summer heat and expands the adjoining rooms. Conversely, to the south, a densely woven brick enclosure simultaneously contains all service areas and provides protection from harsh winter winds.

Contained within galleys—and intersected by a double-fronted open hallway centering a visually porous stairwell—tray slabs in both floors resolve use areas. An intramural open patio is similarly sandwiched within the resulting spatial grid, introducing yet another transitional layer. A parallel sequence of screen walls, containing support functions (fireplaces, closets), defines indoor/outdoor boundaries.

Above and Left: House and pool converse in unity across the stretch of lawn they both flank and define. Set back in the lot, the house assumes a pavilionlike quality in relation to the site.

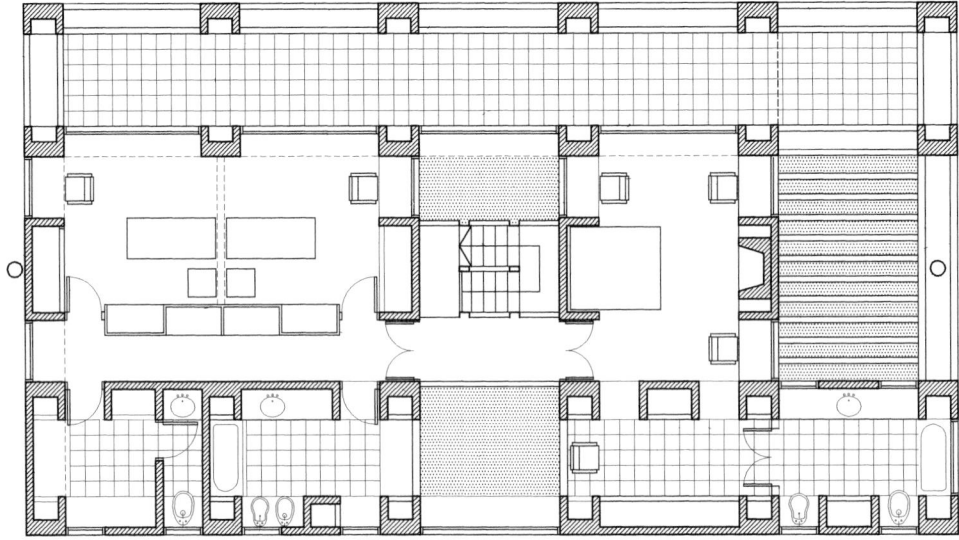

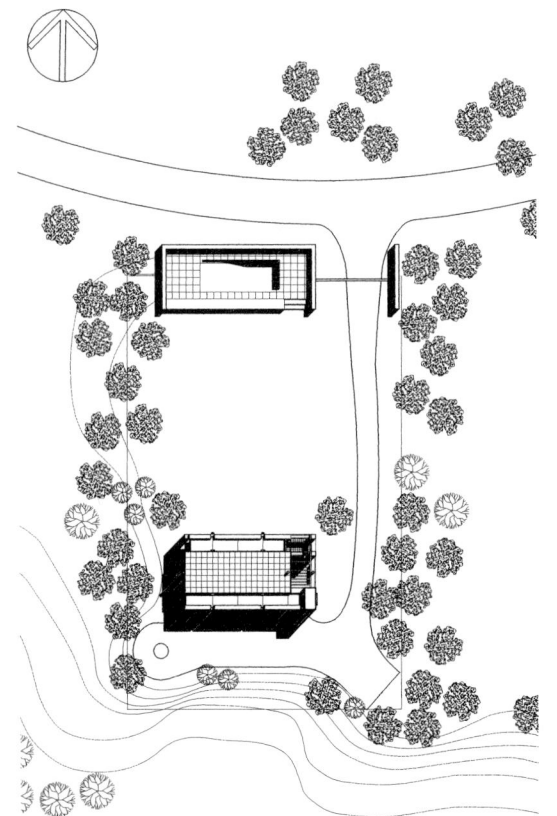

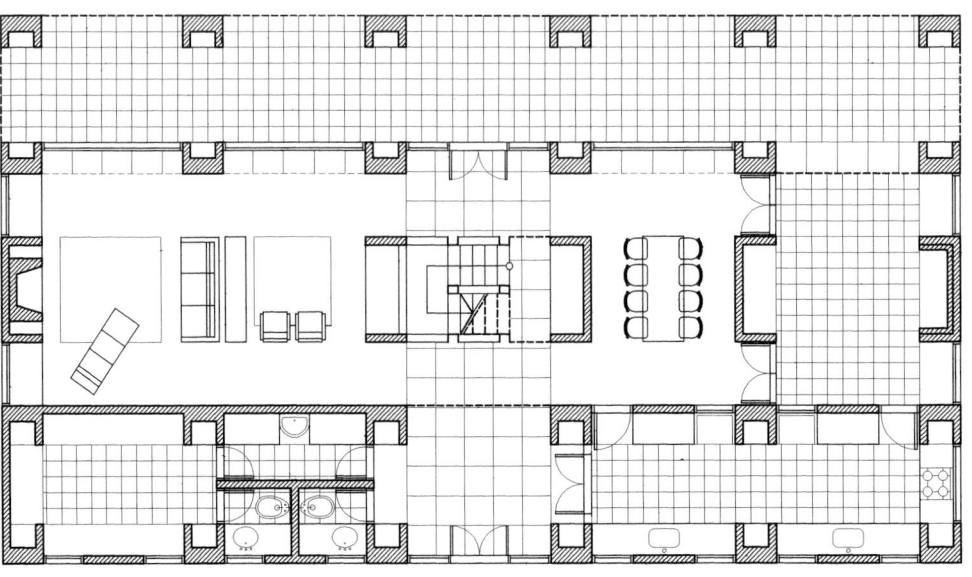

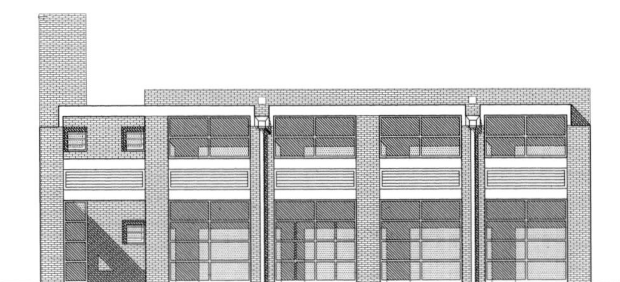

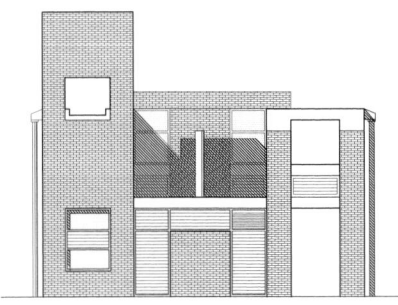

Above: *The sequence of pillars generates a two-tiered verandah, which provides a veritable thermal buffer, conditioned at will by folding shutters and vine-covered jardinieres.*

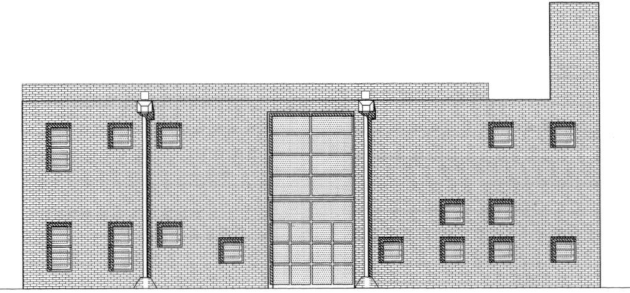

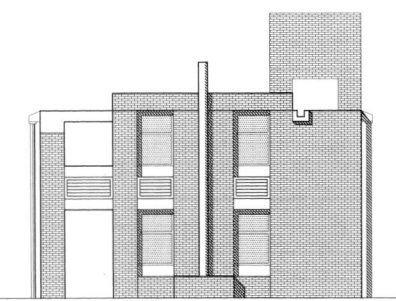

Right: The front galleries, with the continuous white terrazzo floors, provide an alternative living space integrated or excluded at will by a succession of louvers and glass sliders that constitute a double dermis.

Opposite Page: Rising with gridlike precision from the foundation slab, rows of brick pillars define spatial modulation, horizontally bound by floor and roof slabs and permeated by indoor and outdoor atriums.

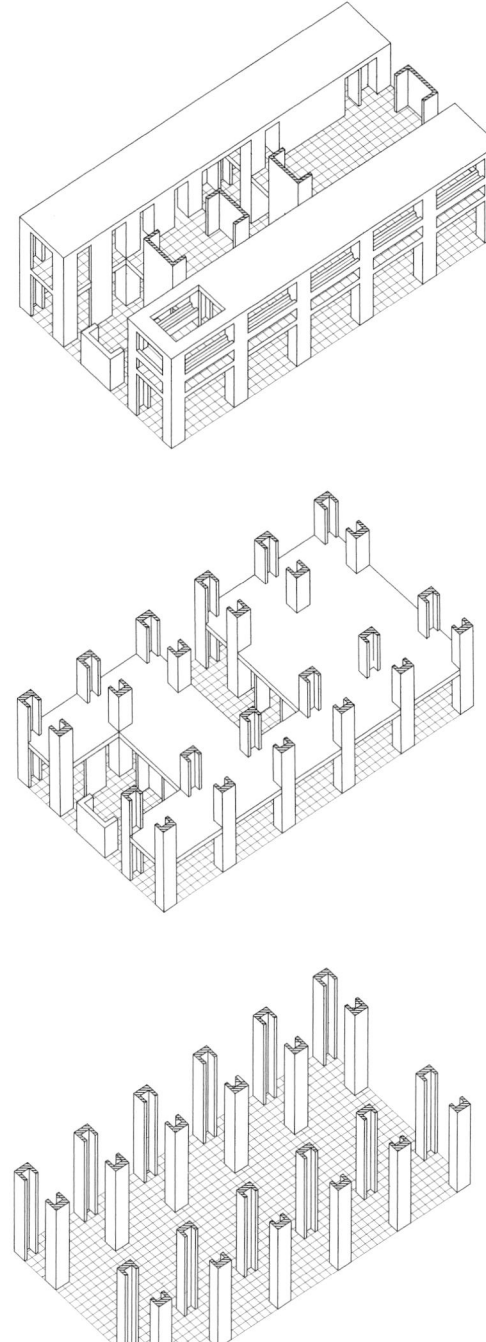

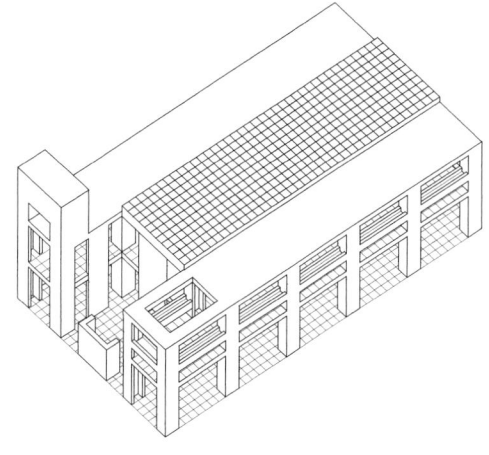

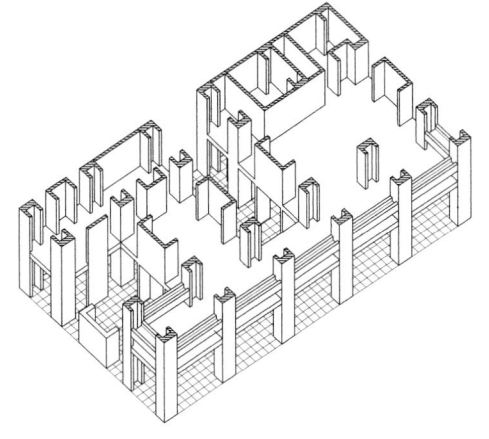

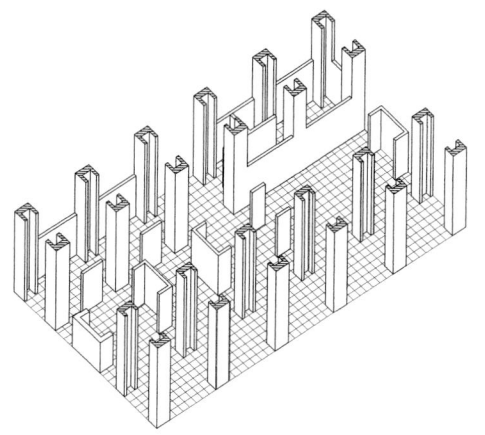

Right: *The extroversion of the of the north galleries is contrasted by the protective hermeticity of the punch-holed South wrapper.*

Opposite Page: *The interconnecting stairs are resolved as a sculptural freestanding steel cage penetrating the core of the house at its center of gravity.*

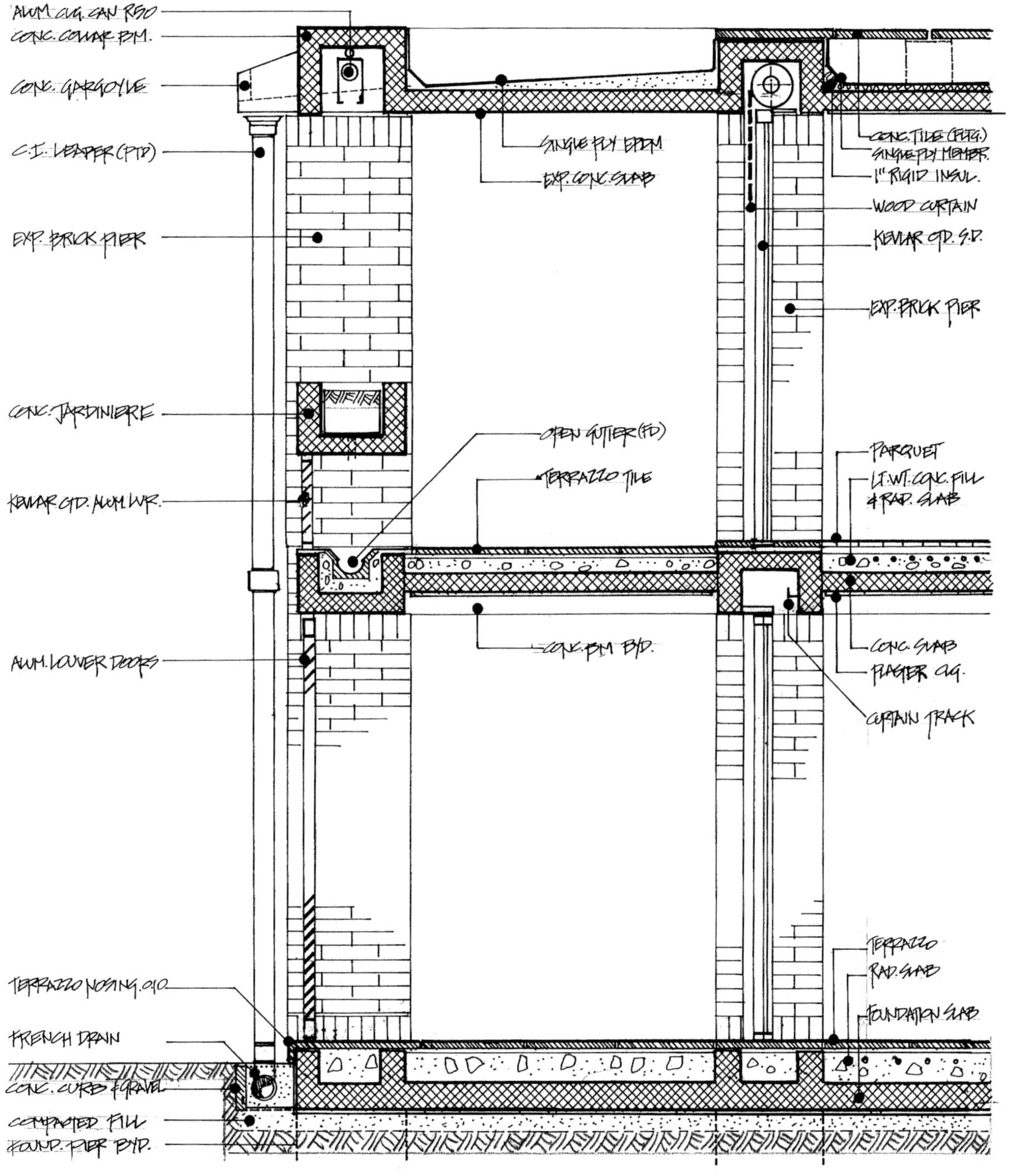

ALUM. CLG. PAN REG.
CONC. COLLAR BM.

CONC. GARGOYLE

C.I. LEADER (PTD.)

EXP. BRICK PIER

CONC. JARDINIERE

KEVLAR GTD. ALUM. LVR.

ALUM. LOUVER DOORS

TERRAZZO NOSING .010

FRENCH DRAIN

CONC. CURB & GRAVEL

COMPACTED FILL

FOUND. PIER BYD.

SINGLE PLY EPDM

EXP. CONC. SLAB

OPEN GUTTER (FD)

TERRAZZO TILE

CONC. BM. BYD.

CONC. TILE (PTG.)
SINGLE PLY MEMBR.
1" RIGID INSUL.
WOOD CURTAIN
KEVLAR GTD. S.D.

EXP. BRICK PIER

PARQUET
LT. WT. CONC. FILL
& RAD. SLAB

CONC. SLAB
PLASTER CLG.

CURTAIN TRACK

TERRAZZO
RAD. SLAB

FOUNDATION SLAB

House in Olivos

Olivos, Buenos Aires, Argentina

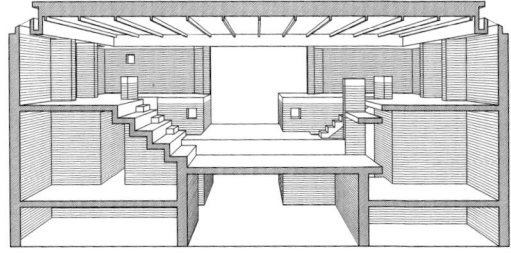

Above and Left: *Exposed brick flanking masses anchor, like propylaea, the fenestrated bridgelike flying deck that resolves social areas under a floating roofline.*

Freestanding in a riverside suburban lot, the Olivos house rises above flood-prone terrain by bridging a multi-level social platform atop service bipodes, themselves under a floating roof deck, all of which reconciles open-plan functionality with vertical layering.

Flanking an open hallway that doubles as car porch on the ground level, exposed brick wrappers of graduated opacity enclose storage and utility crawl rooms, which are tucked under corresponding bedroom stacks and articulated with the central social platform by twin split-level staircases. The staircases seamlessly lead into a loft-like arrangement of open platforms that span the entire floor plan and open themselves onto a wooden deck, reconstructing the garden beyond at parlor level.

Spanning between the rising brick propylaea with carefully orchestrated punch-hole windows, a mirrored succession of wooden French doors flank the bridging loft. This ensures controlled lighting within a thoroughly domestic expressive idiom.

A deep recess separates the wood-ceilinged, corrugated metal roof from bearing masonry. It also conceals gutters and lateral lighting troughs, while accentuating a "floating" effect that visually alleviates a heavily anchored structure. Chimney flues and roof leaders protrude as sculptural icons, from within a heavy blanket of ivy that, crawling over brick, restores a certain degree of linkage to a forgotten site.

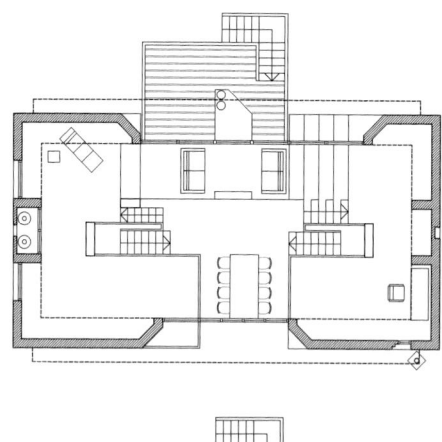

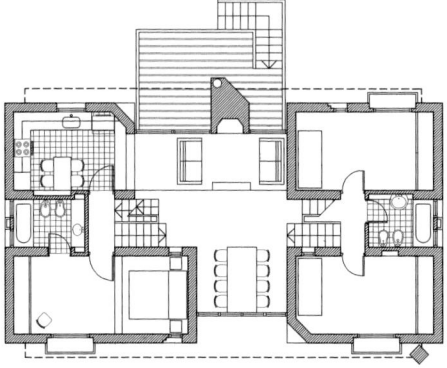

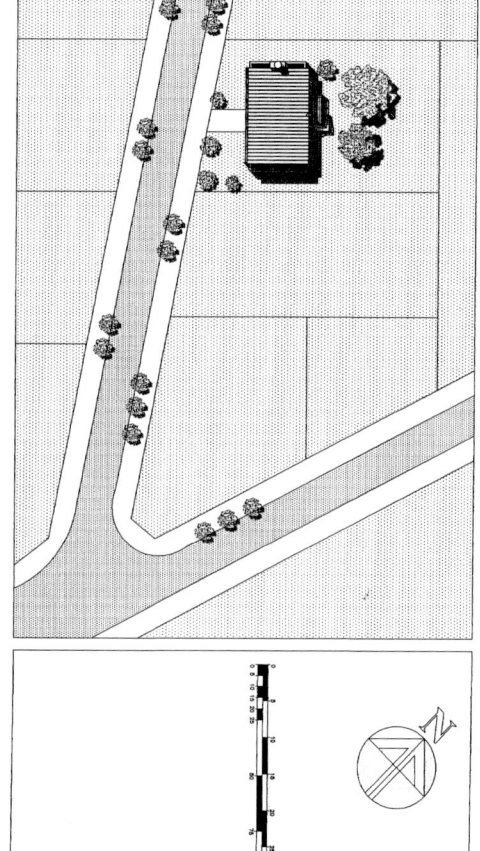

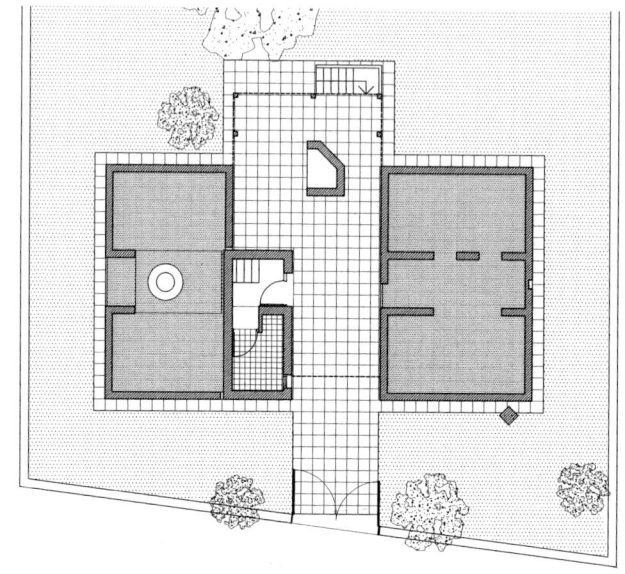

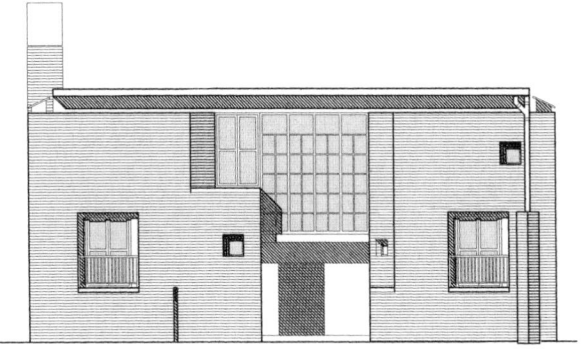

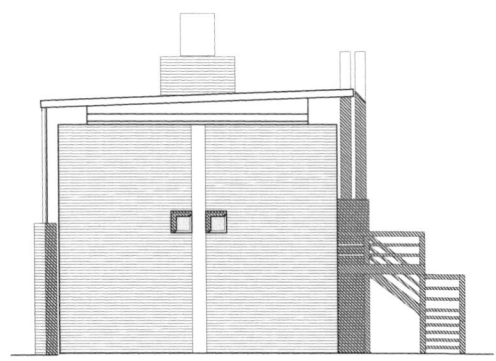

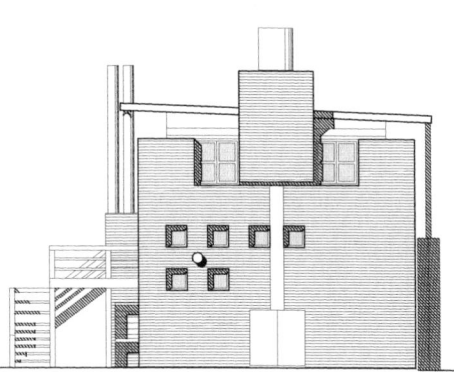

Above Left: *Punch-hole windows and crawling vine alleviate the severity of the brick wrappers, while the exterior wood deck and stairs provide a soft landing to the suspended structure.*

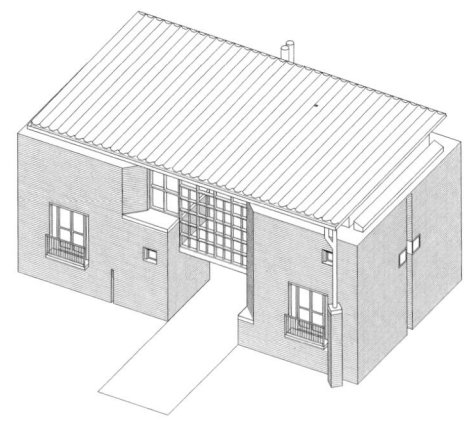

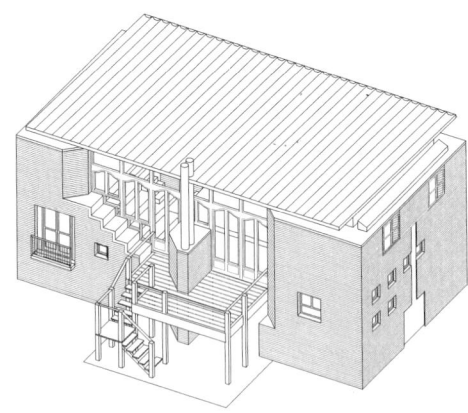

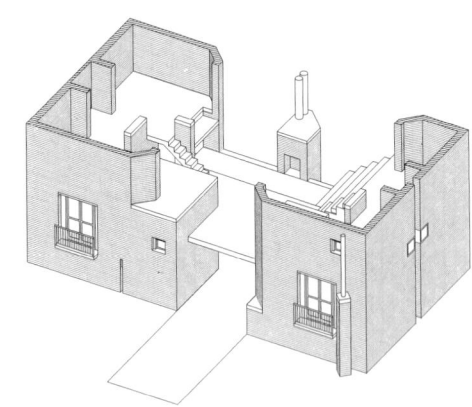

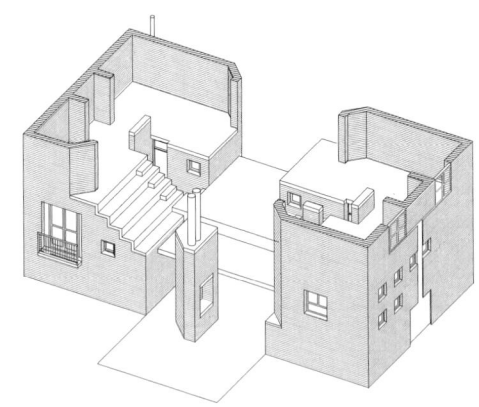

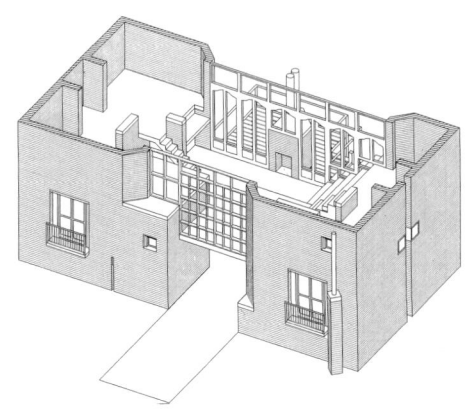

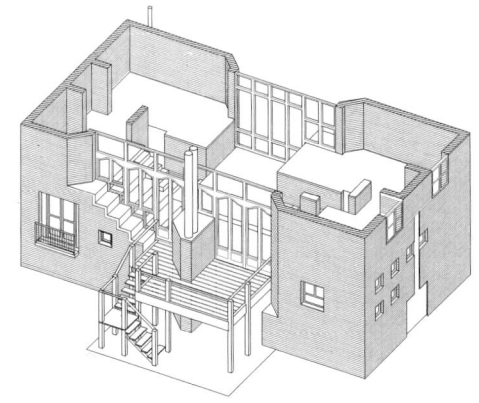

Right: Flanked by an enfilade of salvaged French doors, the seemingly open-plan living areas decompose into a series of terraced platforms that, aided by wall-washing clerestory light penetrations, provide a multi-layered spatial reading.

Opposite Page: The docklike rear stairs provides a detached transition between house and site emphasizing, with its stilt imagery, the flood-prone character of the terrain.

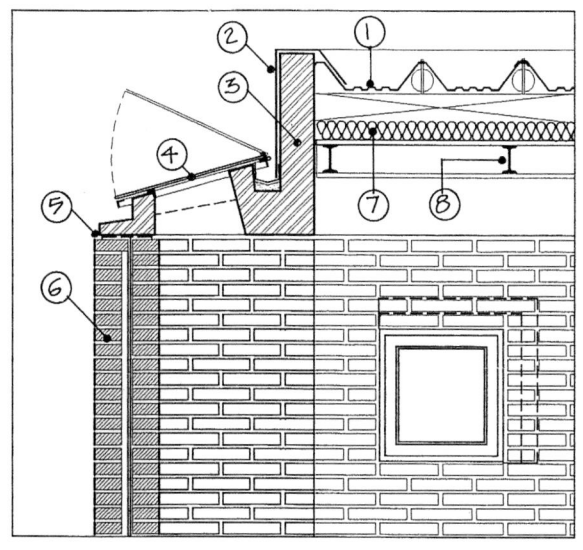
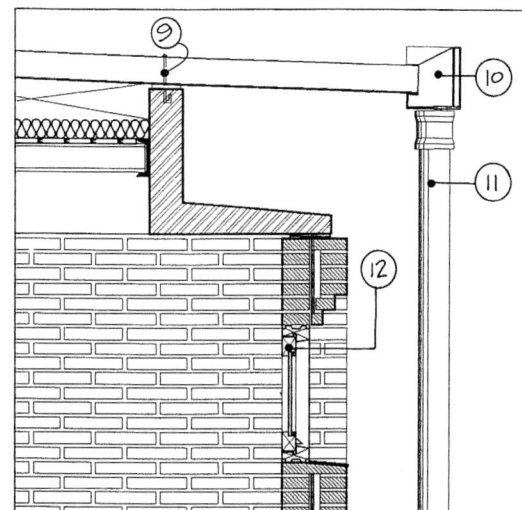
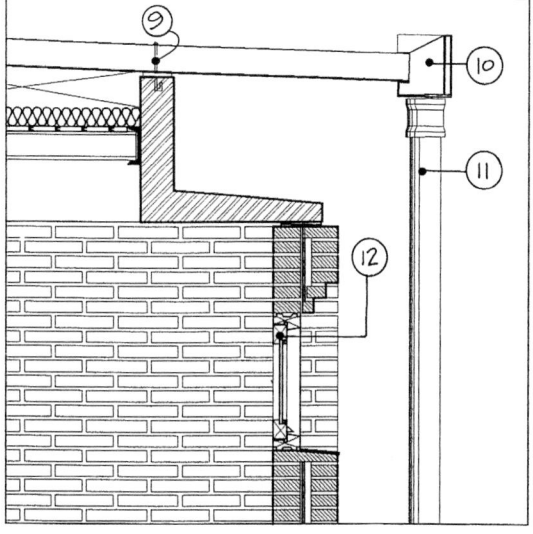
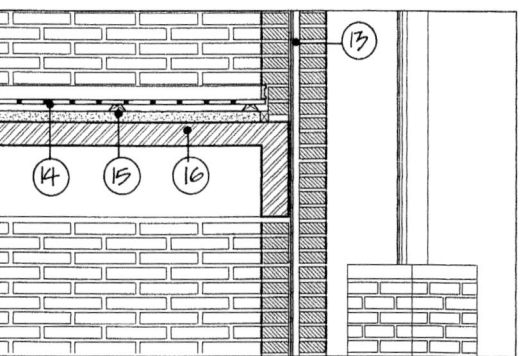

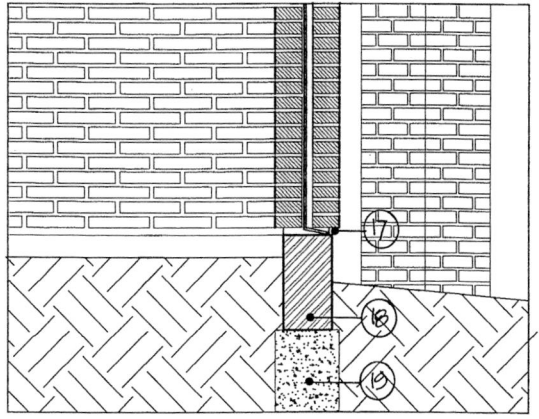

1- GALV. CHANNEL ROOF
2- GALV. COPING + FLASH'G.
3- CONC. COLLAR BM.
4- ST. SKYLITE AWNG.
5- BRG. JOINT
6- BRICK MASONRY (BRG.)
7- R22 BATT
8- STEEL JOISTS (PN1 10)
9- GALV. ANCHOR BOLT (SIL. WASHER)
10- GALV. GUTTER
11- C.I. LDR.
12- WOOD FR. WINDOW UNIT
13- W.P. MEMBRANE
14- 2'¼" PINE FLRG.
15- CANTED SLEEPER
16- CONC. SLAB (EXP.)
17- WEEP HOLE @ 0.60
18- CONC. GRADE BM. 25/40
19- CONC. FOUND PIER (BEYOND)

House in Pilar

Escobar, Buenos Aires, Argentina

Set on an expansively manicured meadow—a stretch of the pampas that has seen wilder days—the Pilar house spans the gap between the traditional working *estancia* and the new culture of suburban weekend retreats. It is an instance of the increasing juxtaposition of urbanity and rurality.

Conceived as exposed brick dice loosely rolled on a green carpet, the massing is axially organized by a glazed "scar" that, traversing the house, articulates social and private areas and constitutes itself into an indoor verandah. Intended to satisfy multiple approaches, the volumetric articulation is strongly perimetral with no single-focus, dominant approach perspective. Entrance atriums, porches, and galleries wedge into volumetric intersections. The interior "walkway," a skylit, two-story longitudinal atrium, feeds laterally disposed areas; they weave through a sequence of orchestrated archways that filter natural light into the enclosed rooms.

The massing deliberately recalls pampas homesteads, including the towering, silo-like corner volume that defines the patio pivoting guest quarters and main house. In concept, the program appears strongly rural; exposed, machine-made brick adds a crispness that bridges the rural and urban dimensions at play. The furnishings, spartan but thoroughly modern, similarly attempt to reconcile both ends of the expressive spectrum.

Above: Freestanding in a sprawling meadow, the house accommodates itself as an articulate amalgam of loosely knit brick volumes, not unlike dice rolled on a carpet.

Left: Bisecting the house lengthwise, a light-filled longitudinal atrium becomes both fracture and scar by articulating with an almost mall-like gathering space the clustered succession of rooms.

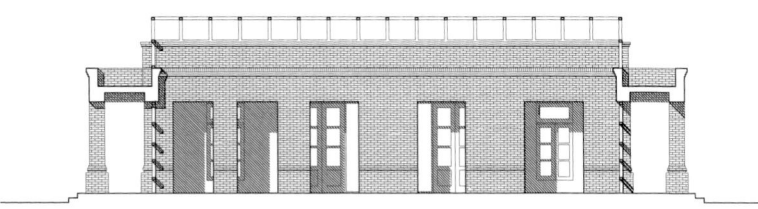

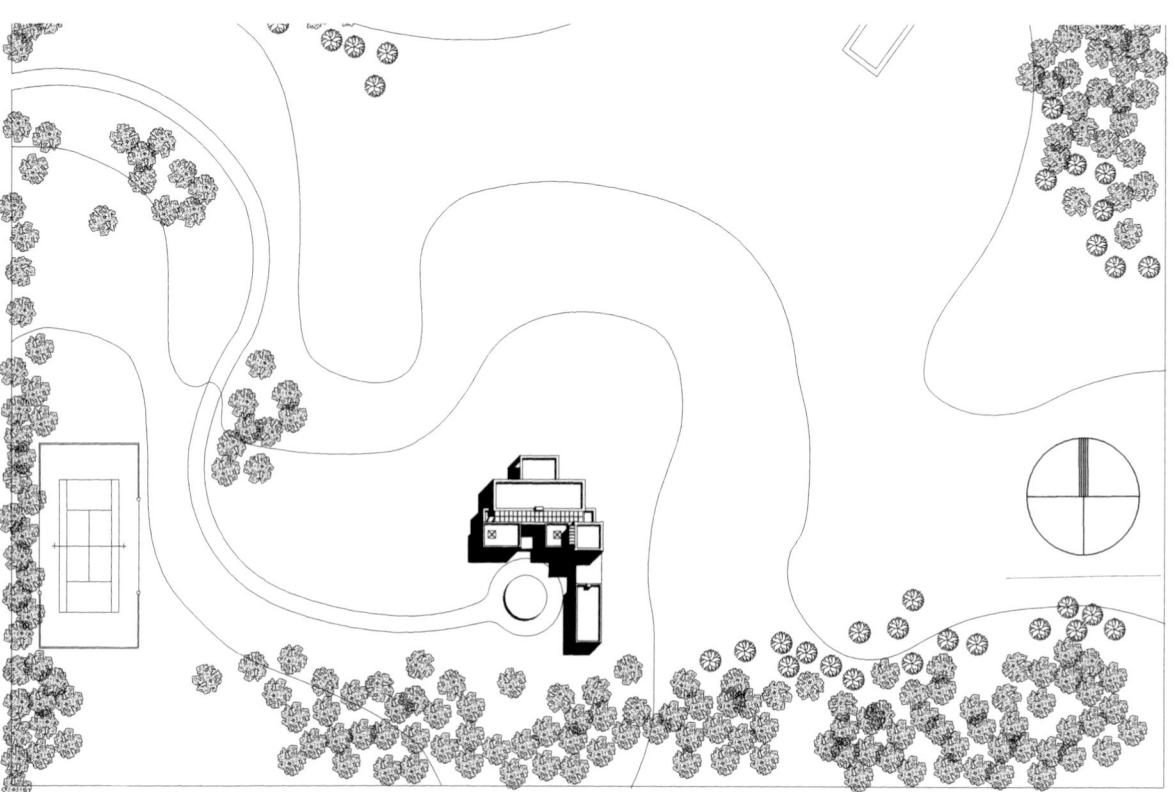

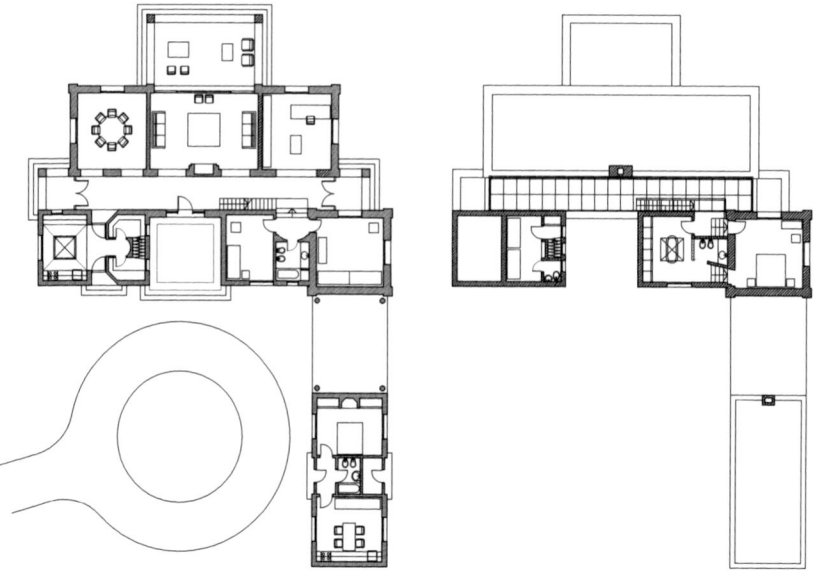

Previous Page: The highly textured, light-washed longitudinal atrium walls contrast the crisp planar qualities of the branching stuccoed rooms.

Right: The starkness of spartan white walls offset by intrusions of exposed brick is underlined by the choice of equally austere furnishings. Urbanity and rurality are squarely confronted.

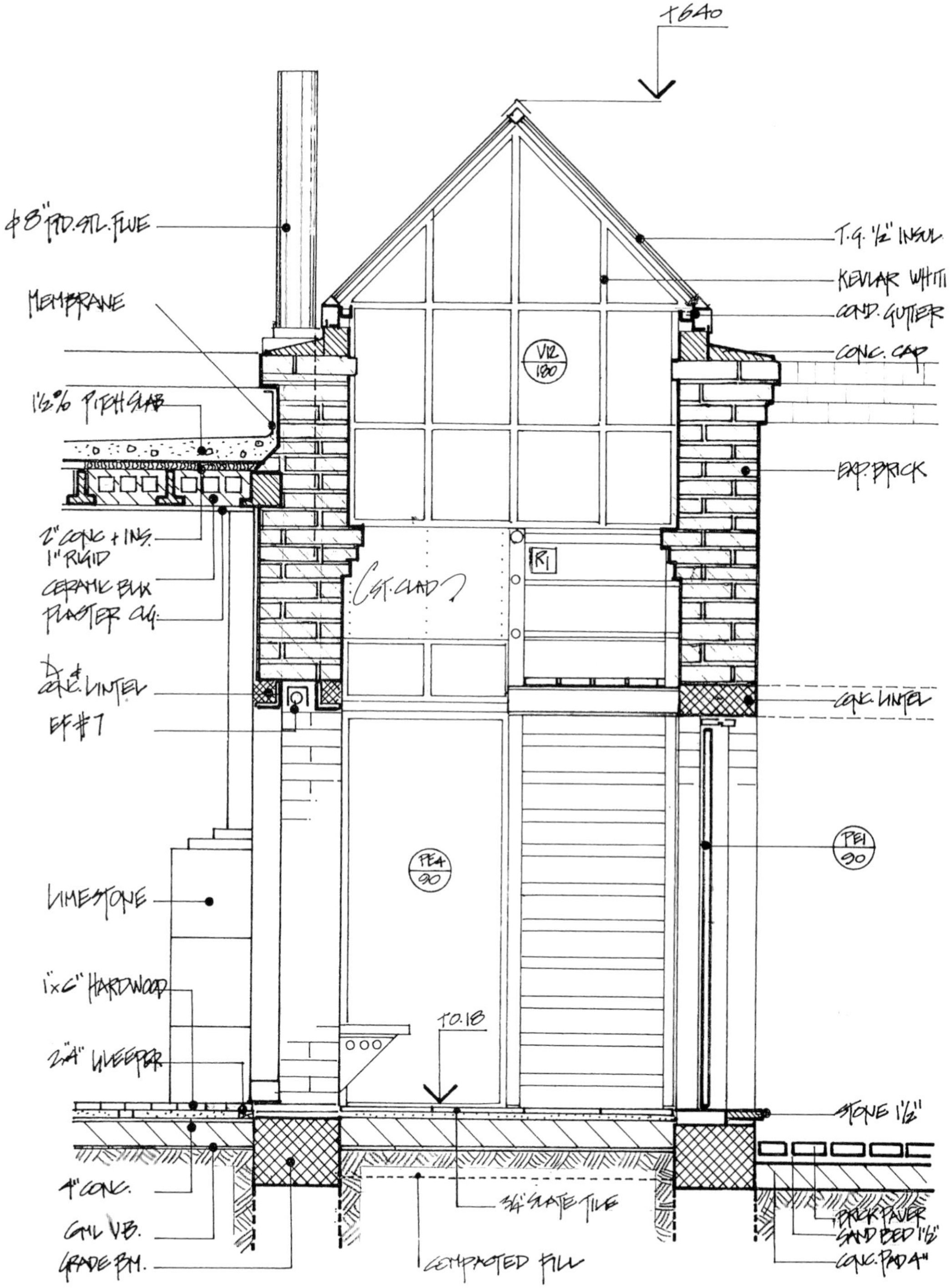

+640

Ø 8" STD. STL. FLUE

MEMBRANE

1½% PITCH SLAB

2" CONC + INS.
1" RIGID

CERAMIC BLK
PLASTER CLG.

D&
CONC. LINTEL

EF # 7

LIMESTONE

1" x 6" HARDWOOD

2¾" WEEPER

4" CONC.

6 ML VB.

GRADE BM.

T.G. ½" INSUL

KEVLAR WHITE

CONT. GUTTER

CONC. CAP

EXP. BRICK

CONC. LINTEL

STONE 1½"

BRICK PAVER
SAND BED 1½"
CONC. PAD 4"

T.O. 18

¾" SLATE TILE

COMPACTED FILL

V12
180

R1

PE4
90

PE1
90

CST. CLAD

House in El Talar

Chascomus, Buenos Aires, Argentina

I n a remote rural setting, at the edge of a swelling marsh and against a backdrop of native *tala* trees, this unassuming *estancia* explores the merging of traditional pampas dwelling typologies with an urban, open-plan lifestyle. This is accomplished through the use of readily available local resources—wood, clay, and rural labor.

The program is decomposed into two conversing architectural entities: the main house and the guest house. The former, containing main living quarters and social areas, resolves as an open-plan, double-galleried enclosure that stretches along the waterfront with a thoroughly horizontal thrust. Pivotal service cores articulate a succession of living areas, punctuated by the rhythm of exposed wooden trusses and piered archways. The latter, condensing accommodations of sporadic use in a vertical silolike layered brick structure, counteracts the horizontal thrust of the main house and helps anchor the compound by defining a time-proven windward patio.

The exposed brick wrapper, doubled up for increased insulation and spatial demarcation, resolves an array of support functions. Its sheer size, punctuated by a succession of linteled bays, creates a light-filtering boundary of humanly scaled space.

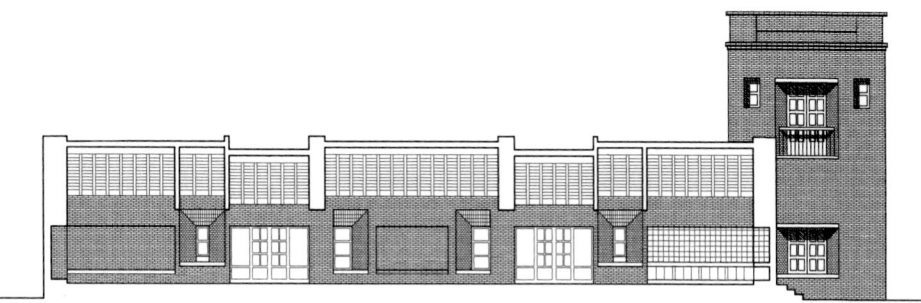

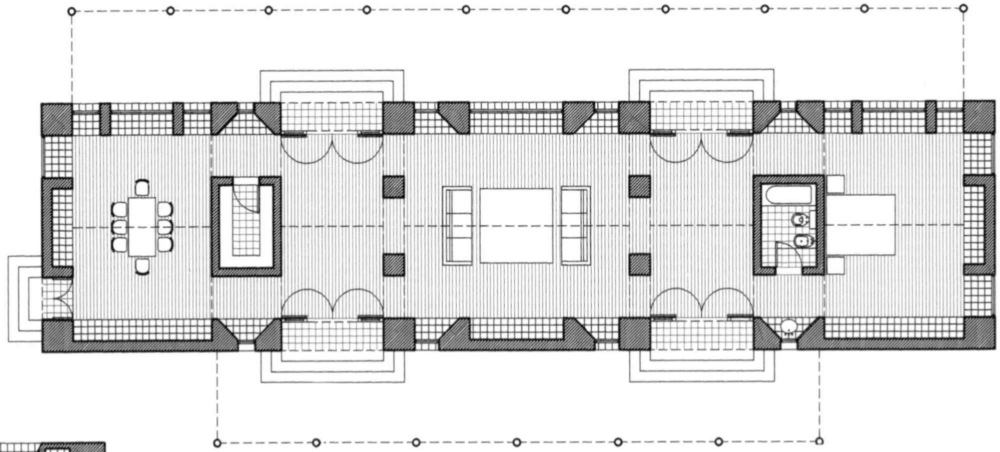

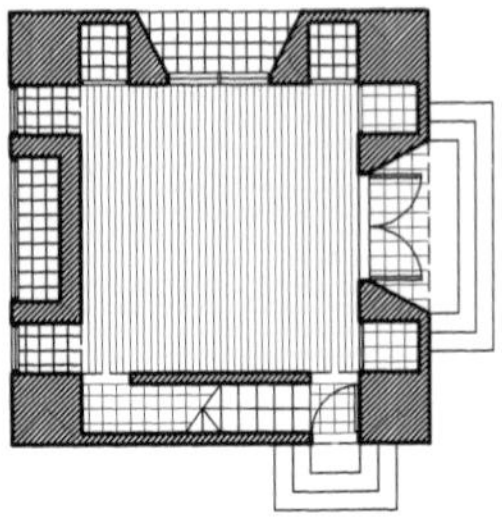

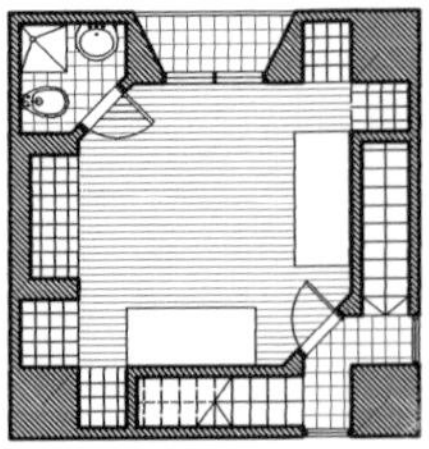

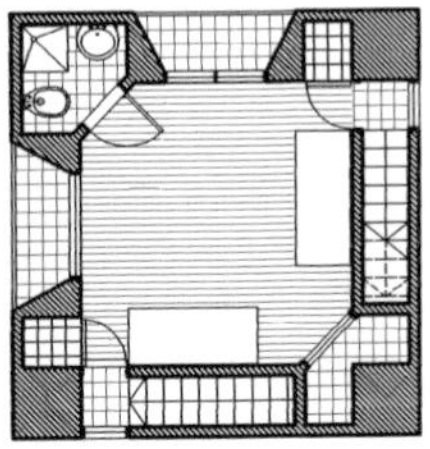

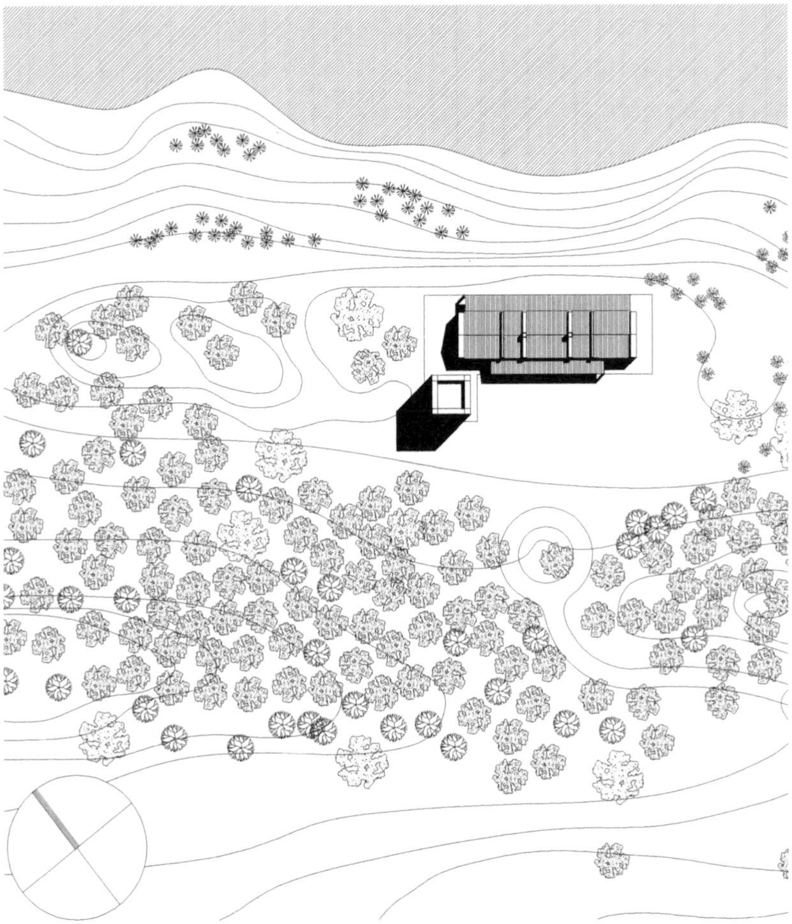

Left: A deep gallery flanks the main structure, providing much needed respite from the harsh summer sun, while reinforcing with the rhythmical punctuation of its steel colonettes the intended expanding horizontality of the compound.

Opposite Page: Deeply set into the folds of the heavily pocketed brick perimeter, thus protected from sun and rain, the fenestration becomes the only expressive recourse within a strictly rational sequence of form and function.

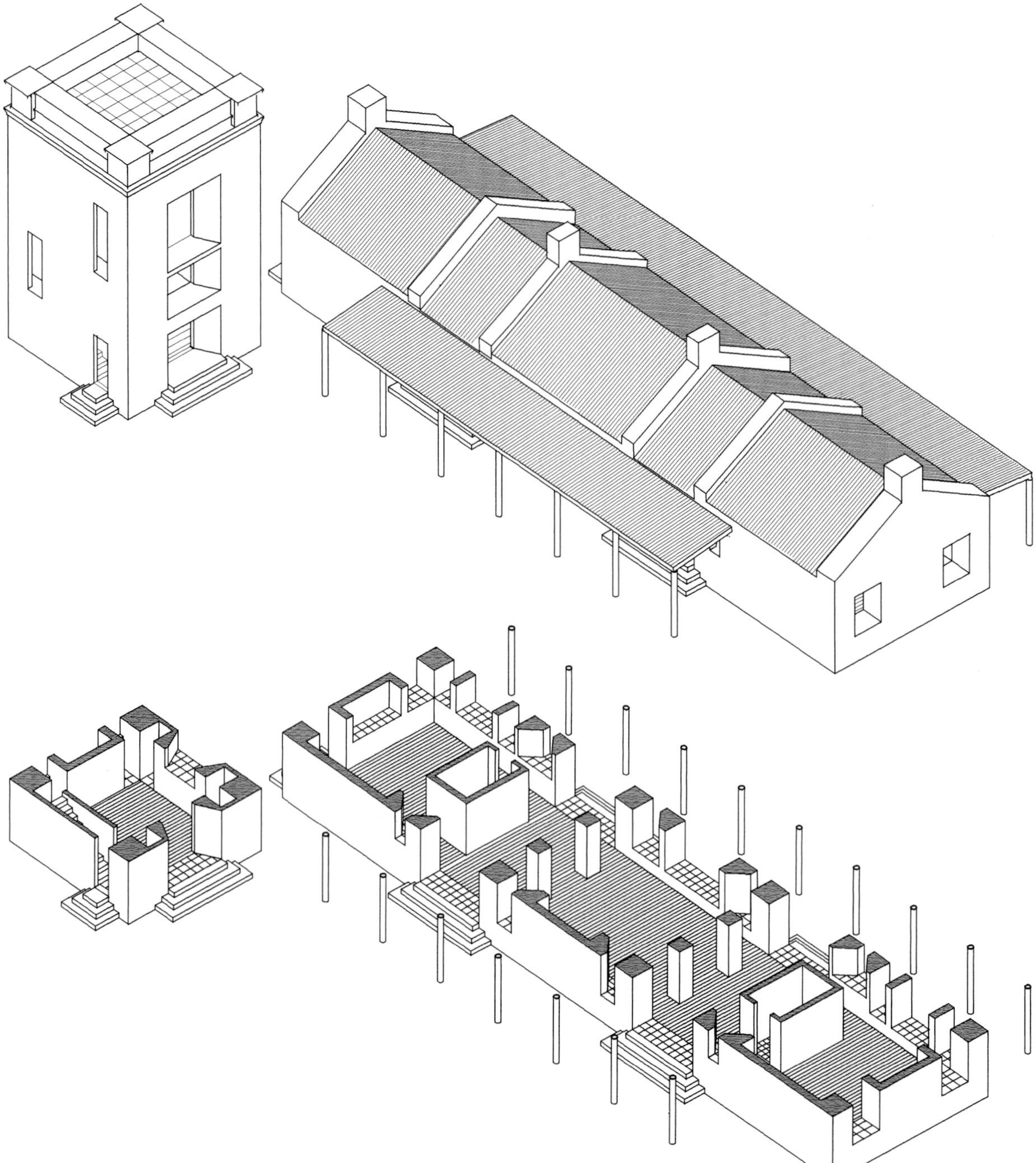

Right: Wood trusses hyphenate the gridlike pattern of the joist and tile ceiling, resting on brick and mortar walls, which acquire an almost sculptural quality as they are successively linteled and carved to incorporate an array of nichelike windows and bays.

Opposite Page: A thoroughly traditional, load-bearing enclosing wall is expanded to incorporate all supporting fixtures—storage, worktops, furnishings, etc.—effectively freeing the open plan arrangement to fulfill its aim: flexibility of use.

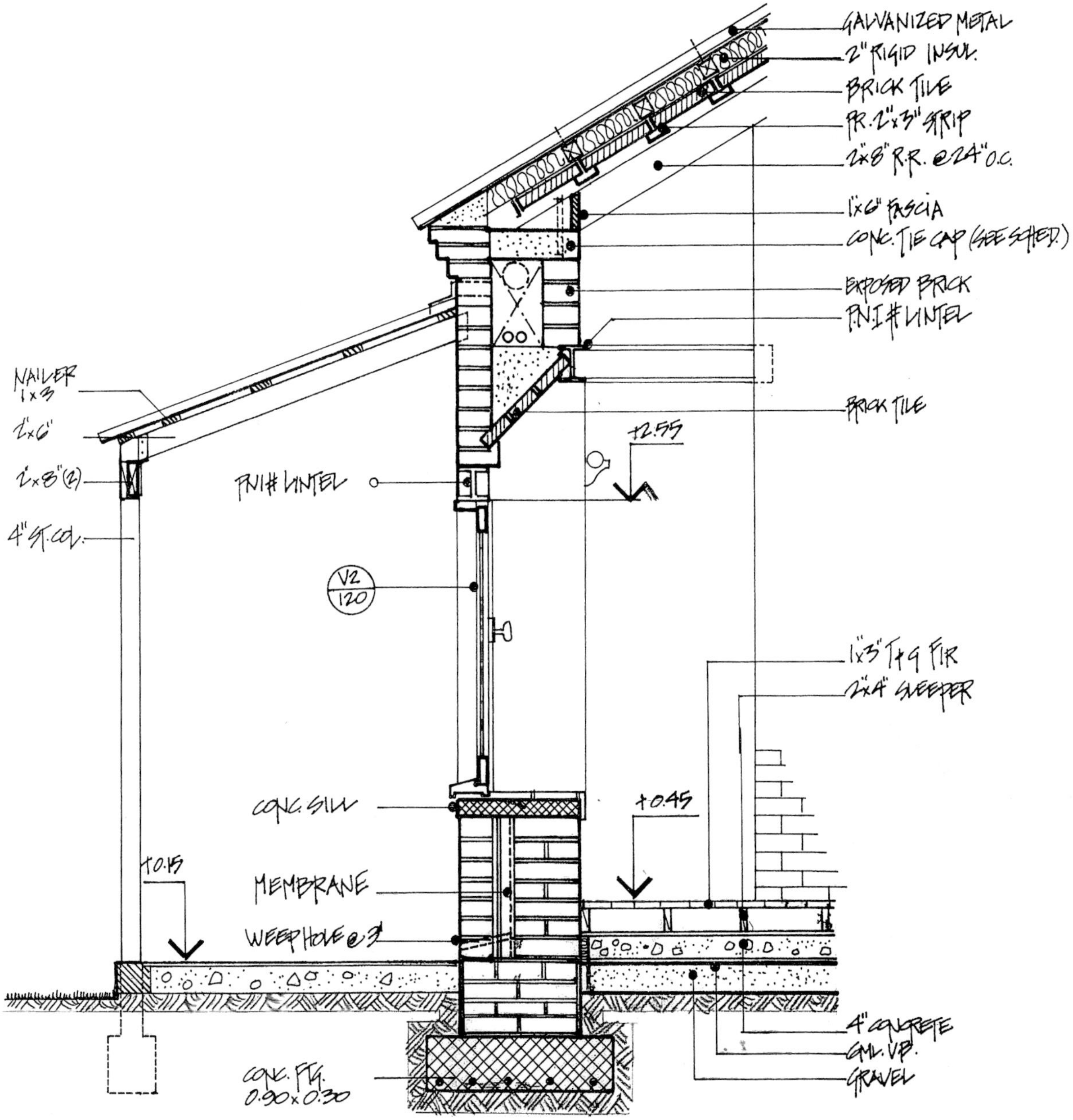

GALVANIZED METAL
2" RIGID INSUL.
BRICK TILE
PR. 2"x3" STRIP
2"x8" R.R. @24" O.C.

1"x6" FASCIA
CONC. TIE CAP (SEE SCHED.)

EXPOSED BRICK
P.N.I. # LINTEL

BRICK TILE

NAILER
1"x3"

1"x6"

+2.55

2"x8" (2)

PNI # LINTEL

4" ST.CQ.

V2
120

+0.15

1"x3" T&G FIR
2"x4" SLEEPER

CONC. SILL

+0.45

MEMBRANE

WEEP HOLE @ 3'

4" CONCRETE
GVL. VB.
GRAVEL

CONC. FTG.
0.90 x 0.30

House in El Salado

Rio Salado, Buenos Aires, Argentina

Set on a stretch of windswept flatland, enclosed by a sharp bend in the Salado River—a typically meandering pampas waterway—this house's unorthodox program solves the lodging needs of three closely attached—yet highly individual—family members. Privacy, interaction, and flexibility to absorb changes in family structure and dynamics were thus resolved in a parti linking three open-plan, self-sufficient modules articulated by deliberately residual expansion buffer wedges that run along a wrapping walkway surrounding a common green. This effectively reconstructs the centrifugal, open patio of the early *estancias*.

Each module is fully resolved, dug into a sloping, continuous berm of merging land and grass-covered rooflines, which deflect dominant winds, echo the river embankment, and fuse site with building. A succession of repetitive brick facades—carefully fenestrated for maximum sun exposure—recreates the quasi-urban scale of provincial rural hamlets along the brick-paved sidewalk, defining a highly ambiguous architectural setting. A staccato of vine-covered pergolas along said walkway defines both the individual expansion areas of each module and the sense of communal space that reconstructs family life alongside the homestead patio.

Hand-molded brick, locally available and readily understood, becomes the expressive vehicle throughout, the coarse detailing—cornices, eyebrows, socles—the resulting imprint of gracefully naive second nature technology.

Above: *Site and object melt into each other, the grassy river berms inching up the rooflines and vice versa.*

Opposite Page: *The succession of repetitive modular facades around a common green introduces a degree of urbanity and community to this definitely rural compound. Crawling vines, however, are a reminder that Nature reigns.*

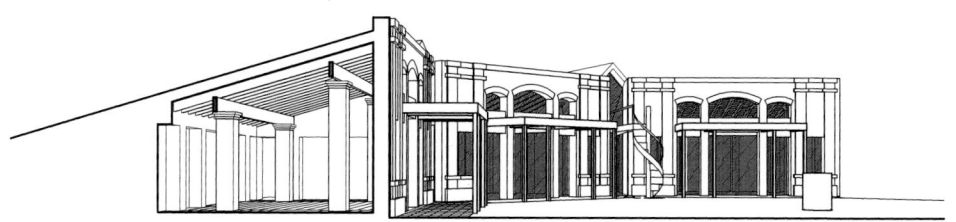

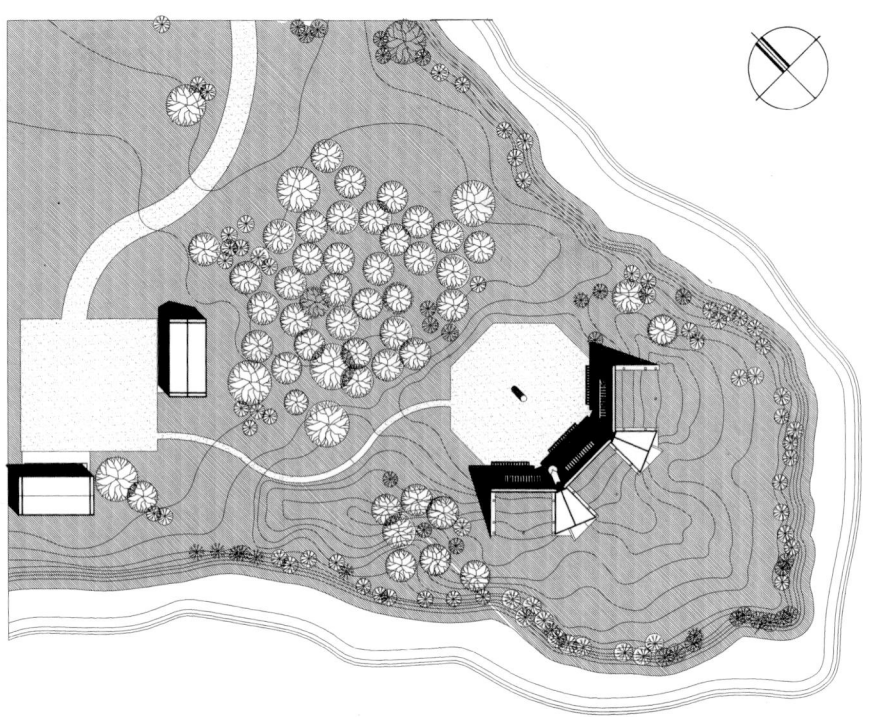

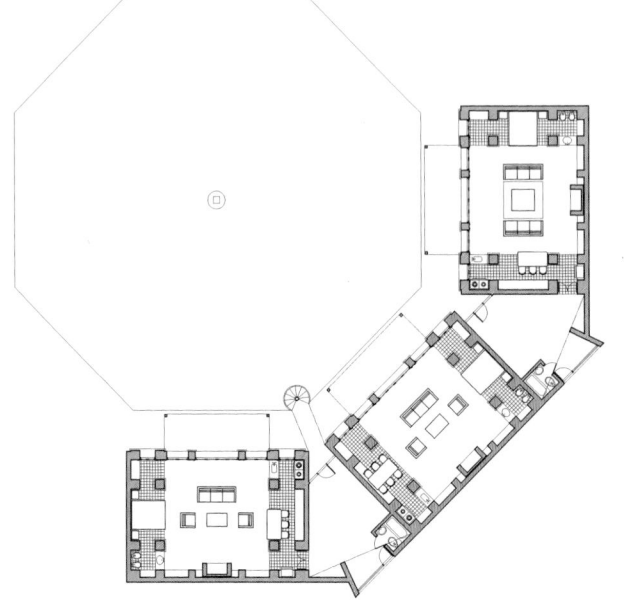

Left: *Conventional masonry detailing, free-flowing from the worker's hand, caps the severity of a screenlike facade, pierced by a succession of French doors and softened by vine-covered pergolas that both delimit private space and establish communal continuity.*

Opposite Page: *Freestanding against the vast horizontality of the pampas, the sequential repetition of almost theatrical facades infuses a sense of urbanity which, loudly and proudly spells out "settlement," in a direct reference to the early pioneers of rural Argentina.*

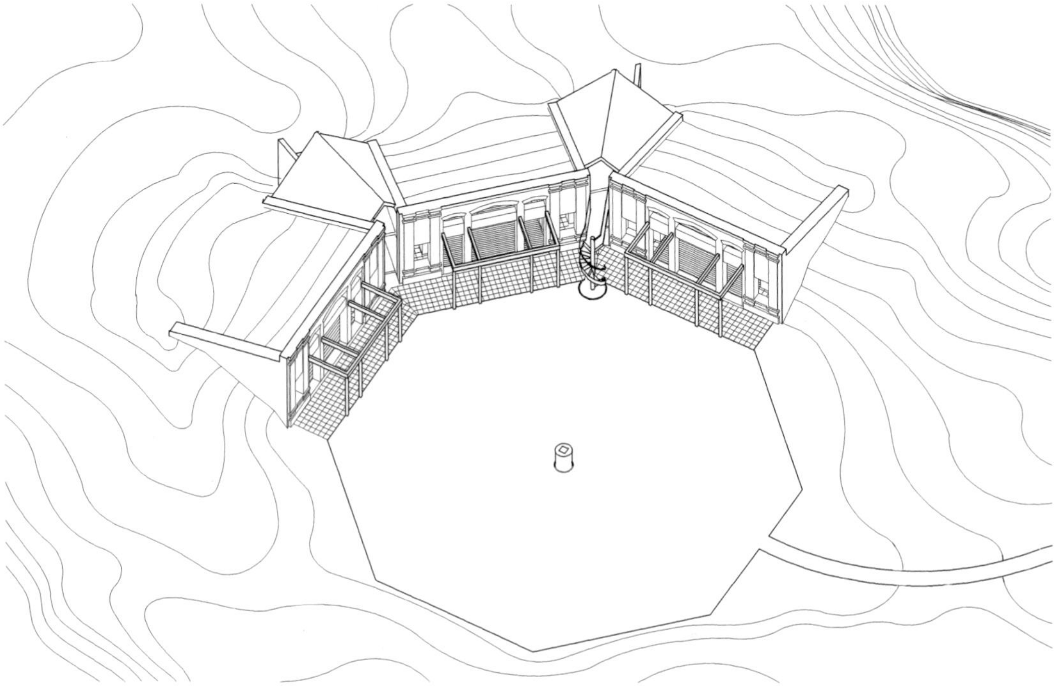

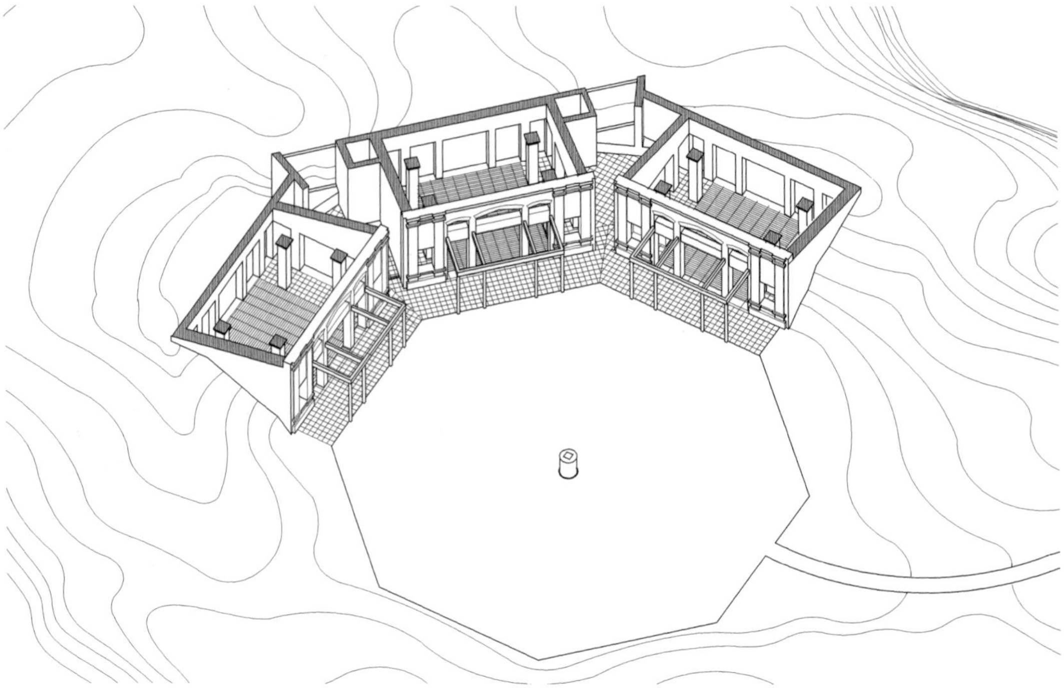

Right: *The centrifugal open plan is punctuated by perimetral brick piers, in turn delineating private and service areas within the wraparound enclosure.*

Opposite Page: *Resting on a water-filled foundation slab and snugly embraced by grass-covered earth berms, each module relies on the precise angling and fenestration of its north wall in order to maximize exposure benefits.*

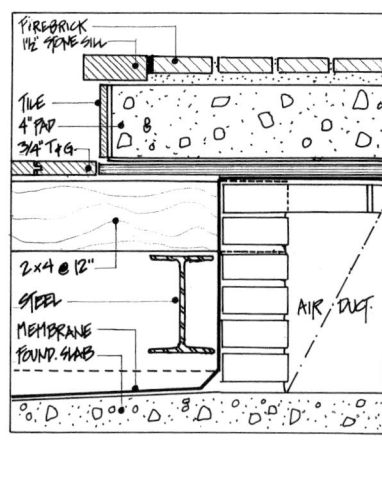

1. FLOOR DRAIN
2. FOUNDATIN SLAB (SHELL AGGREGATE)
3. WATERPROOFING/ VB
4. HORIZONTAL VENT
5. STEEL JOIST-PNII 16
6. VENT DUCT
7. 3"X3" NAILER
8. 1"X4" HARDWOOD FLOOR
9. EXP. BRICK PIER 0.52X0.52

10. 4"X4" GIRDER
11. 3"X8" @0.60 R.R
12. 1"X3" SLEEPER
13. BRICK
14. CONC. SLAB (SHELL AGGREGATE)
15. CEMENT FLATBED
16. MEMBRANE (9 PLY BUILT-UP)
17. SOIL 0.20
18. SMOKE FLUE

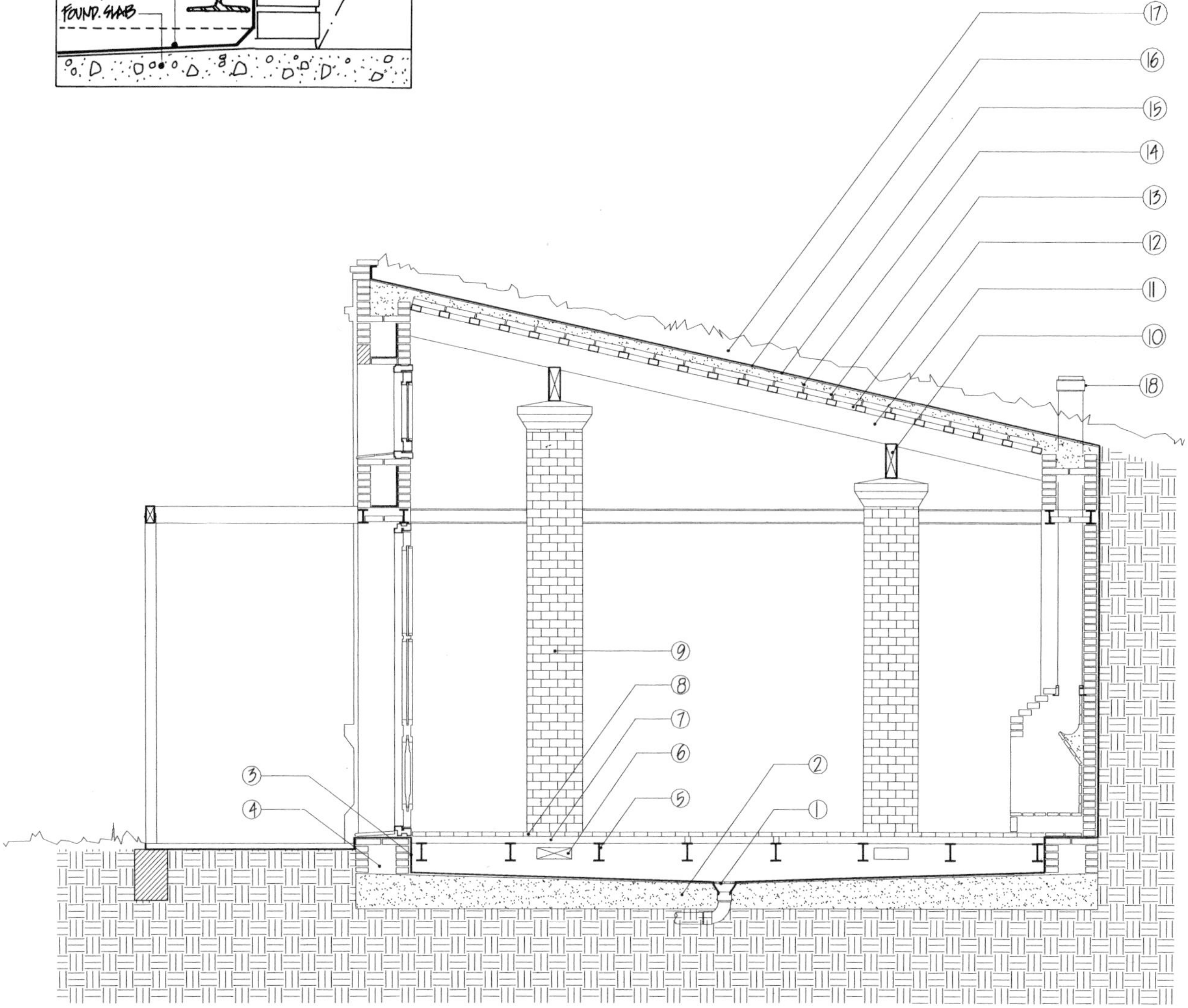

House in San Martin

San Martin de los Andes, Neuquen, Argentina

C antilevered off the Andean mountain face and tucked under a grass-covered, concrete kerchief, this wooden deck—wedged into a crevice—translates the basic physical and spiritual needs of refuge into built form, spelled out by a simple program in a harsh environment.

In an attitude of deliberate self-denial, the shelter turns its back on those who approach it. A parochial shingled turret protrudes from a blanket of grass, the only discernible sign of its existence. Instead, it opens itself onto the abyss beyond. A wood-mullioned curtainwall, angled so as to maximize sun penetration and shade projection, barely demarcates spatial boundaries and defines the one recognizable architectural element in this effacing non-building. Sandwiched between roof shell and floordeck, the "house" lacks any other interior plane of reference. Exposed rock becomes the spatial wrapper.

Towering in center stage, the Russian stove, a wood-fed firebrick source of radiant heat and hot water, becomes the only recognizable orthogonal spatial fulcrum in this otherwise grotto-like structure. Personal needs—bathing, sleeping—are symmetrically sidelined into the roof folds, concealed by floating screens and storage units. Spartan furniture and a few objects sprinkled at random, by their sole presence, transcend utility and become strongly referential.

Above: For all its bravado, the humble shingled entryway, which doubles as a thermal flue, is the only indication of a house's existence to the unaware approaching visitor.

Left: Solidly anchored into the Andean rock, the grass-covered refuge emerges vigilant over the Valley beyond.

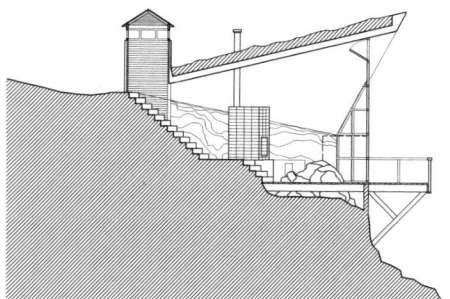

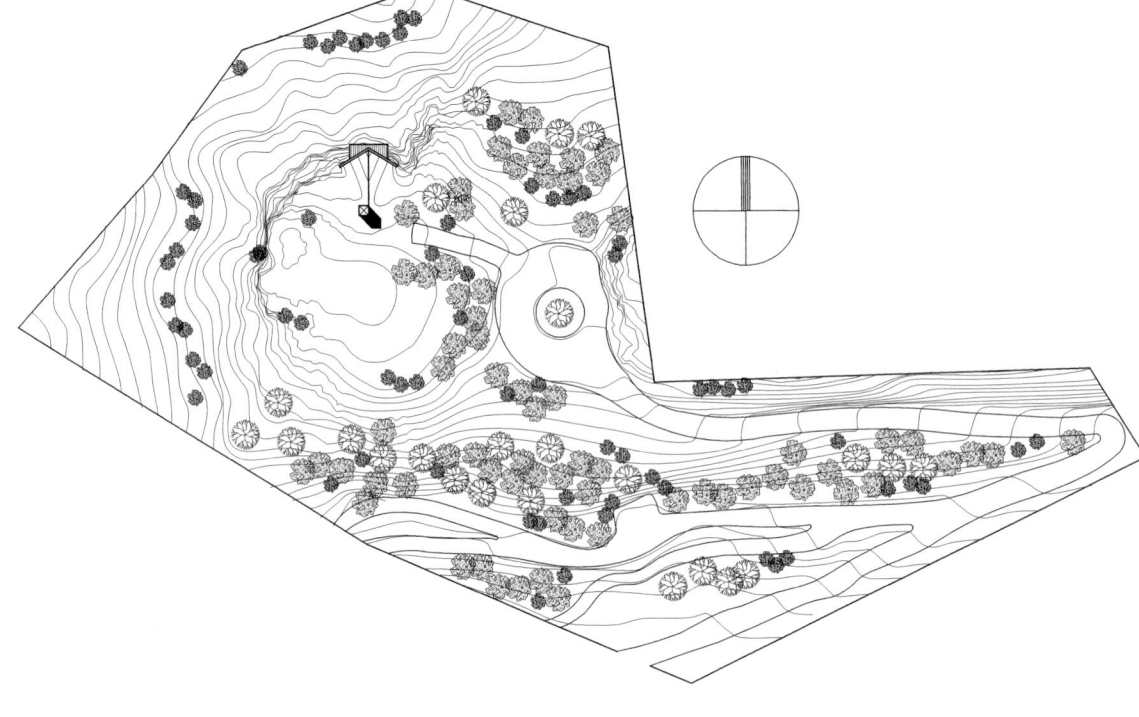

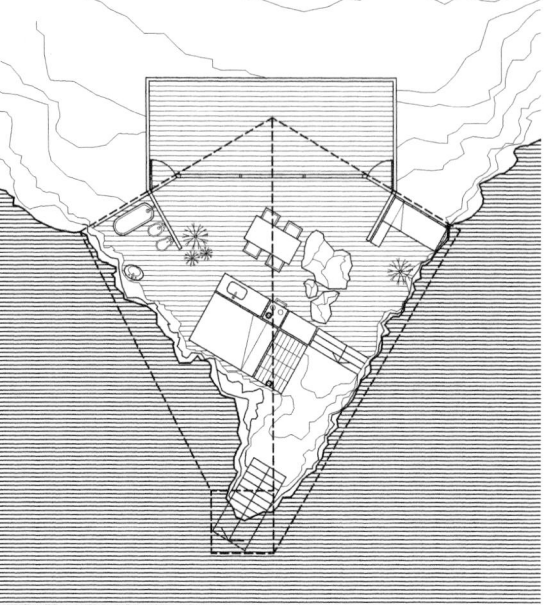

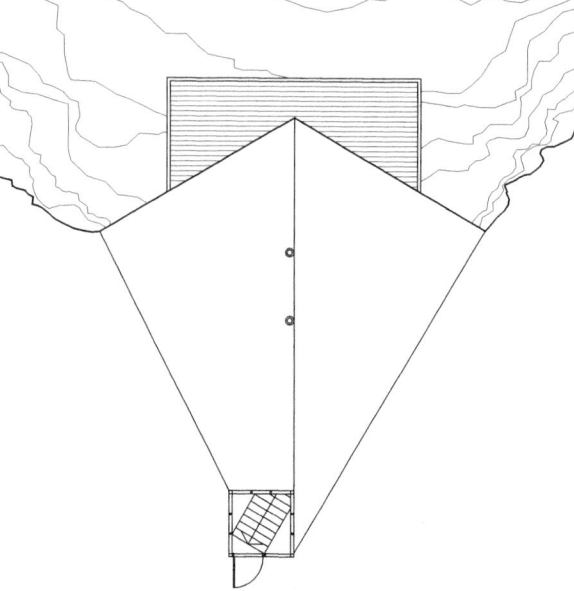

Left: *Simultaneously assertive and submissive, the house's geometry is both emphasized and tamed by nature.*

Opposite Page: *Not unlike an architectural Jekyll and Hyde, the shingled turret is the unassuming counterface of the proudly jutting, sparkling trapeze.*

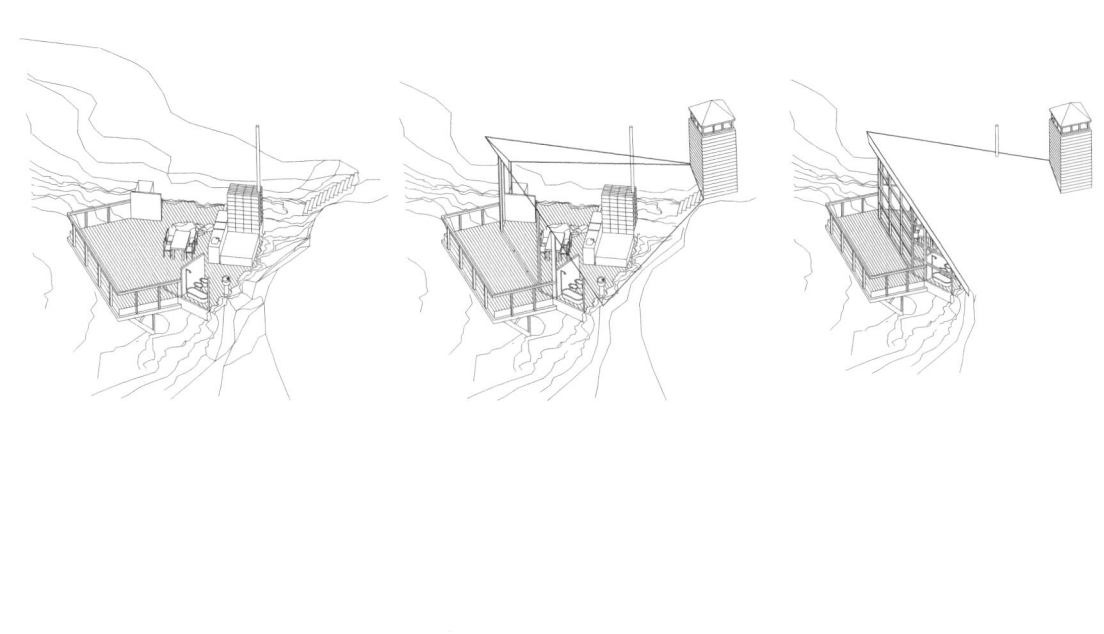

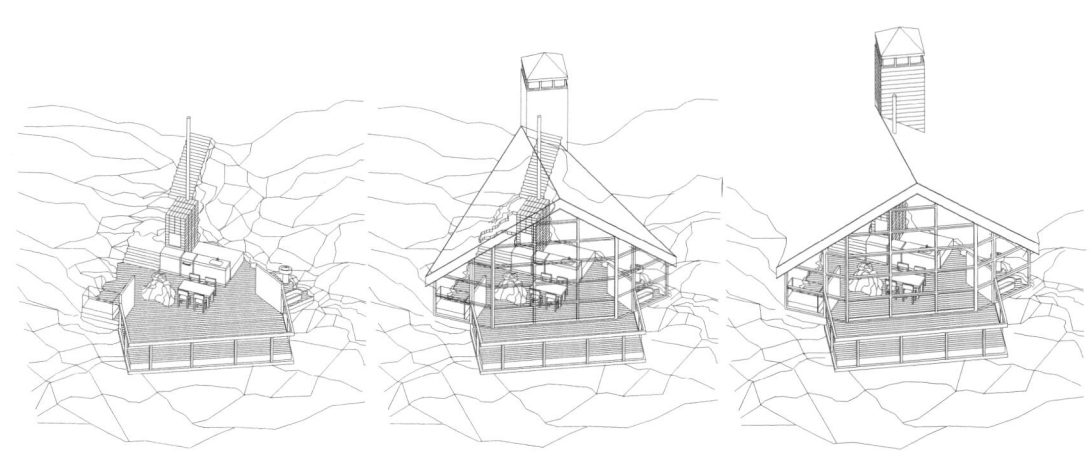

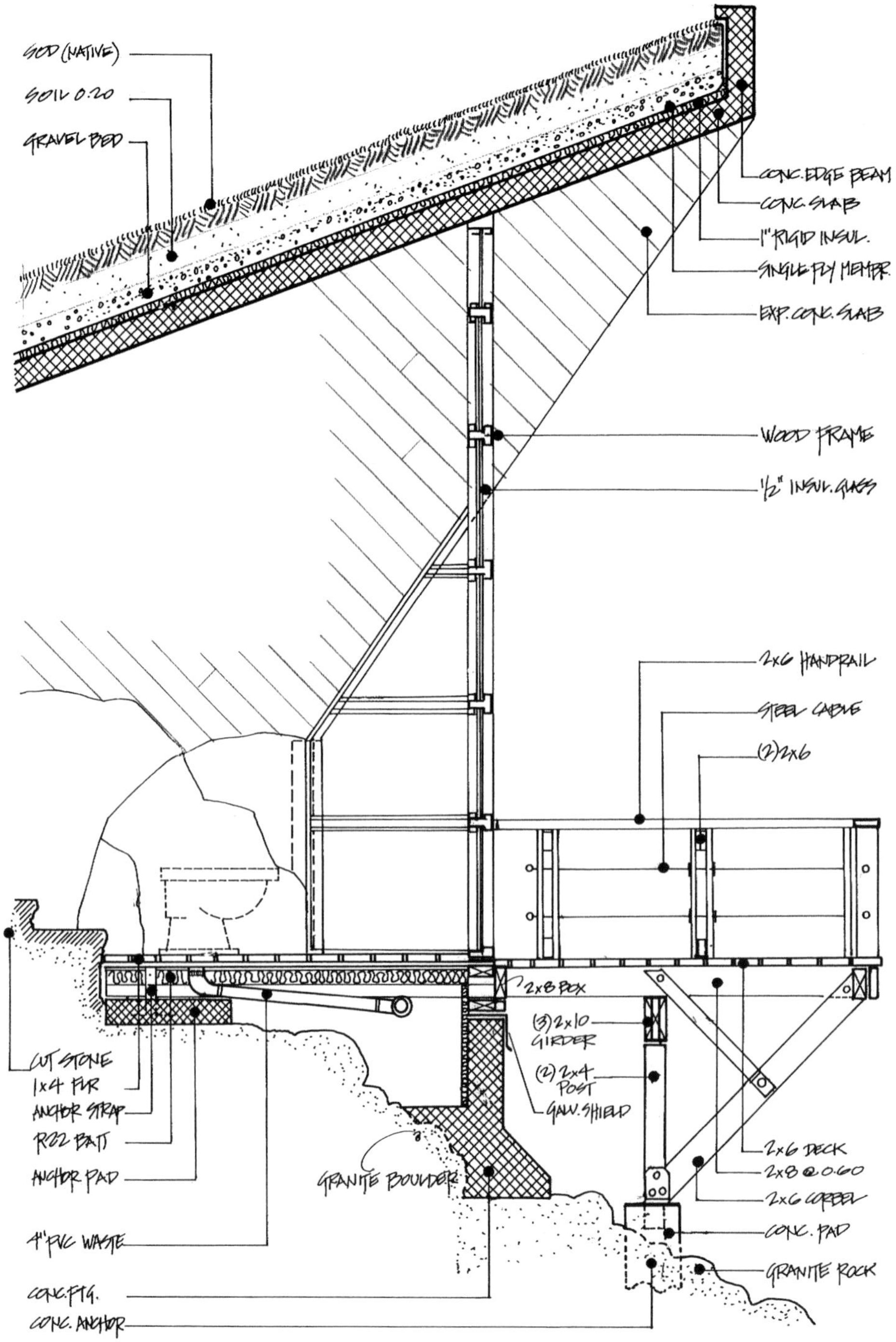

SOD (NATIVE)

SOIL 0.20

GRAVEL BED

CONC. EDGE BEAM
CONC. SLAB
1" RIGID INSUL.
SINGLE PLY MEMBR.
EXP. CONC. SLAB

WOOD FRAME

1/2" INSUL. GLASS

2x6 HANDRAIL

STEEL CABLE

(2) 2x6

2x8 BOX

(3) 2x10 GIRDER

(2) 2x4 POST
GALV. SHIELD

2x6 DECK
2x8 @ 0.60
2x6 CORBEL

CONC. PAD

GRANITE ROCK

CUT STONE
1x4 FLR
ANCHOR STRAP
R22 BATT
ANCHOR PAD

GRANITE BOULDER

4" PVC WASTE

CONC. FTG.

CONC. ANCHOR

Selected Buildings and Projects

House in San Isidro

San Isidro, Buenos Aires, Argentina

Site: 16,000 sf

Building: 3,500 sf

Date of Design: 1981

Construction Completed: 1982

House in San Martin

Neuquen, Argentina

Site: 2 acres

Building: 800 sf

Date of Design: 1983

Construction Completed: 1983

House in El Salado

Rio Salado, Chascomus, Argentina

Site: 2.5 acres

Building: 3,400 sf

Date of Design: 1984

Construction Completed:

Phase 1–1985, Phase 2–1988

House in El Talar

Chascomus, Buenos Aires, Argentina

Site: 2.5 acres

Building: 3,200 sf

Date of Design: 1985

Construction Completed: 1986

House in Pilar

Escobar, Buenos Aires, Argentina

Site: 1.5 acres

Building: 3,800 sf

Date of Design: 1989

Construction Completed: 1990

House in Olivos

Olivos, Buenos Aires, Argentina

Site: 4,400 sf

Building: 2,200 sf

Date of Design: 1984

Construction Completed: 1985

House in Cabrer Alley

Buenos Aires, Argentina

Site: 2,400 sf

Building: 2,400 sf

Date of Design: 1987

Construction Completed: 1989

House in Gorriti Street

Buenos Aires, Argentina

Site: 4,000 sf

Building: 2,400 sf

Date of Design: 1990

Construction Completed: 1991

House in Carranza Street

Bueno Aires, Argentina

Site: 4,400 sf

Building: 1,800 sf

Date of Design: 1994

Construction Completed: 1994

House in Maine

Kittery, Maine, USA

Site: 1.8 acres

Building: 1,800 sf

Date of Design: 1995

(Project)

Lacroze Miguens Prati Architects

1975–1995

Eduardo Lacroze, AIA

Jose Ignacio Miguens

Francisco Prati

Pablo Iglesias Molli

Gonzalo Aulet

Eduardo Bellocq

Maximo Bush Frers

Carolina Daverio

Cesar Doretti

Quique Dourge

Alvaro Farina

Julian I. Gomez

Sergio Gorelik

Fernando Iglesias Molli

Ramon Iglesias Molli

Joaquin Iglesias Molli

Daniel Jove

Carlos Lopez Achaval

Miguel Angel Mansueto

Ricardo Monti

Daniel Morita

Edgardo Regatky

Taco Rey

Marcela Riva

Sebastian Robirosa

Antonia Robirosa

Peter Rolih

Cuki Sojo

Andres Vigerna

Firm Profile

Established in Buenos Aires in 1975, the architectural partnership of Eduardo Lacroze, Jose Ignacio Miguens and Francisco Prati has undertaken to date a vast and varied range of projects—residential, commercial, institutional—in a wide array of countries in South and Central America. The firm established a practice in New York in 1989.

Active in the fields of architectural, interior, and furniture design, the firm has been recognized with a number of distinguished awards, notably the Buenos Aires Biennale CAYC Gold medal and the Sofia, Bulgaria, Interarch Silver Medal, the SCA Annual Architecture Citation, and an AIA Award Commendation in 1993. It also won a number of architectural competitions, most recently the renovation and expansion of the 1906 Stanford White premises of the Argentine Consulate in New York City.

Lacroze Miguens Prati's works are published in Argentina, Chile, Brazil, and Colombia; they are exhibited in museums and institutions in Buenos Aires (CAYC, Centro Cultural San Martin), Sao Paulo, Santiago de Chile, New Orleans (Municipal Auditorium, Armstrong Park) and Chicago (Chicago Atheneum). All three principals remain active in the academic world, teaching, lecturing, and writing (Universidad de Buenos Aires, CAYC, Royal Danish Academy, Revista Summa, Arkitekten). *Summa,* the doyen of Latin American professional journals, devoted a full issue on the firm; the School of Architecture of the Universidad de los Andes in Bogota, Colombia, included the work of Lacroze Miguens Prati in a comprehensive survey of trend-setting, Latin American architecture and the Italian journal *Abitare* has prominently featured the firm in its recent review of Argentina's architectural landscape.

Although the bulk of the work is centered on larger scale housing and resort projects, the humble yet resourceful houses in this book fully represent the design attitude prevalent in the firm's architecture; they provide the best examples of how a small—but focused—practice confronts a wide range of design challenges in changing contextual conditions.

Eduardo Lacroze

José Ignacio Miguens

Acknowledgments and Credits

Associate Firms

Hugo Andaloro, Architect, *House in Olivos*

Medici-Puente-Trucco, Architects, *La Pedrera, Uruguay*

Julian I. Gomez, Architect, *House in Pilar*

Laura Orcoyen, *House in Pilar*

Fernando Hermann and Enrique Cordeiro, Architects, *House in El Talar*

Fahsen-Vela, Architects, *Guatemala*

Fahsen-Vela, Architects, *Hotel Camino Real-Tikal, Guatemala*

Reynaldo Archbold, Architect, *Hotel Decameron, San Andres Island*

Calmaquip Engineering, Miami, *Hotel Decameron, San Andres Island*

Special Thanks

Luis Maurette, Architect

Michael Rubenstein, AIA (NY)

Manuel I. Net, Architect

Photographic Credit

Gustavo Sosa Pinilla

Models

Roberto Bendinger

Ramon Iglesias Molli